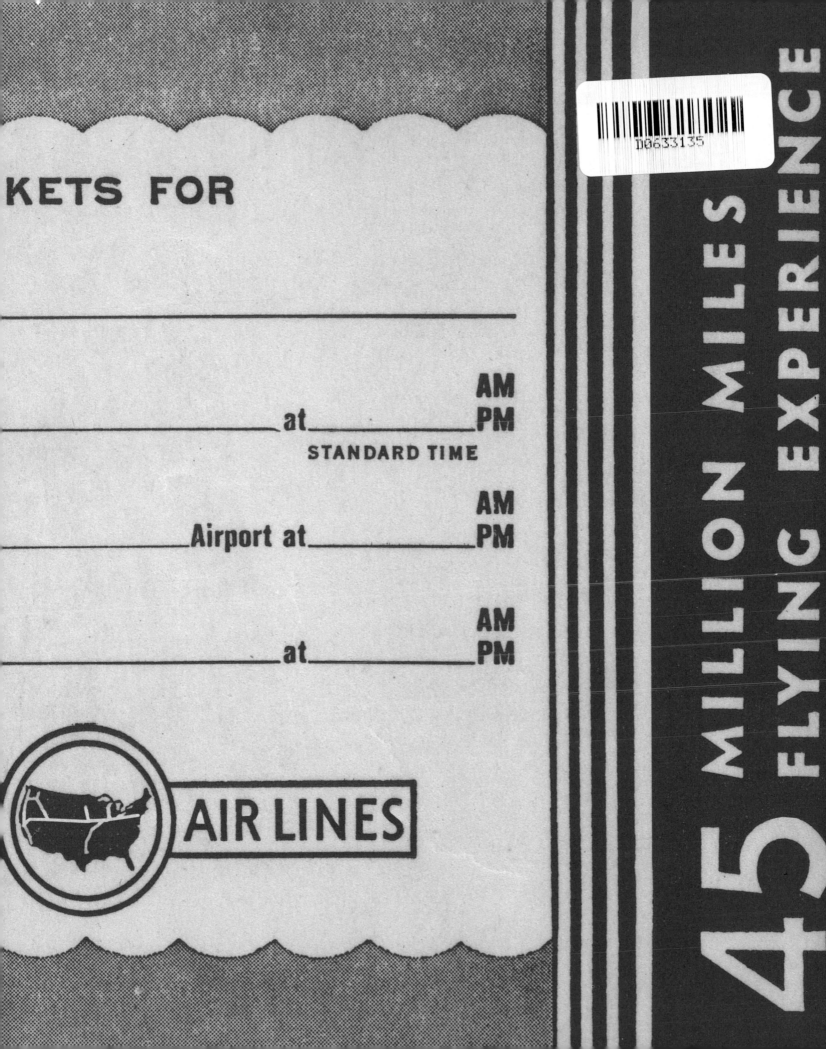

KETS FOR

_____

_____at _____ AM PM
STANDARD TIME

_____ Airport at _____ AM PM

_____at _____ AM PM

AIR LINES

45 MILLION MILES FLYING EXPERIENCE

THE AGE OF FLIGHT

A History of America's Pioneering Airline

By William Garvey & David Fisher

A core group of daring early airmail pilots got United off the ground. Jack Knight (center, legs crossed) *became a legendary United captain.*

CREDITS & ACKNOWLEDGMENTS

Library of Congress Control Number: 2001131120 / ISBN 0-9667061-1-0

RANDY JOHNSON . . . Editorial Director / Contributing Author

LISA FANN, ALICIA MILLER, SPENCER CARNEY, BEN ANDERSON, SELBY BATEMAN, JEFF GRIFFIN,

COLLEEN MARBLE, KAREN MILHOLLAND, DENA SCOTT-CAULDER, BILL MARSANO . . . Pace Communications Editorial Team

JAIMEY EASLER . . . Design / Art Director

JENNIFER HILL . . . Assistant Art Director

JAMES A. DeCATA . . . Production Director

BONNIE McELVEEN-HUNTER . . . President and CEO, Pace Communications, Inc.

BARB HANSON . . . Coordinator / United Archives

ADRIAN DELFINO . . . Former United historian / historical consultant

JOHN COOPER and the other retiree volunteers of United Archives

BARBARA GAM . . . Editor / United Employee Communications

DONNA SITKIEWICZ . . . Director / United Communications Services

The authors and Pace Communications wish to extend a special thanks to United's Barb Hanson. Her dedication to
this project—and the rich history of United Airlines—made the undertaking possible. Barb's unflagging energy and expertise on behalf
of this book and the United Archives have ensured the survival of an inspiring piece of aviation's past. We also gratefully thank
Adrian Delfino and photographers Michael P. Masuka, Chris Sorensen, and Wayne Slezak for their contributions.

Pace Communications, Inc., 1301 Carolina Street, Greensboro, NC 27401, www.pacecommunications.com
Prepress by American Color, Nashville, TN / Printing by QuebecorWorld, Kingsport, TN

In 1935, United employees posed proudly with a new Boeing 247, the first modern airliner, at Chicago Municipal Airport (now Midway).

TABLE OF CONTENTS

Mechanics inspect the engines of a DC-3 Mainliner during a routine visit to United's Cheyenne, Wyoming, overhaul base in the late 1930s.

A bird is an instrument working according to a mathematical law. It lies within the power of man to make this instrument ... such an instrument fabricated by man lacks nothing but the soul of man. —LEONARDO DA VINCI

WINGS OF DESIRE | 13

IT HAD BEEN THE DREAM OF MANKIND FOREVER—TO RISE FROM THE EARTH, SOAR THROUGH THE SKIES, AND RACE THE clouds. From the beginning of invention, men of learning had searched for the secrets of flight.

In the Middle Ages, the first brave adventurers climbed to the tops of castle towers carrying wings of cloth and leaped into the air—only to fall back to Earth. By 1500, the mysteries of flight had captured the imagination of Leonardo da Vinci, who sketched several ornithopters, flying machines with bird-like wings that flapped up and down when powered by foot pedals. The wings of da Vinci's fanciful flyers were covered by canvas, but these craft were much too heavy to rise from the ground.

It was more than two centuries later that man finally flew. In June of 1783, while the United States was in its infancy, the French Montgolfier brothers successfully demonstrated a hot air balloon. In September of that year, King Louis XVI and Marie Antoinette watched with awe as the lighter-than-air craft, fueled by a smoky fire of chopped wool and straw, rose heavenward from a courtyard at Versailles carrying a sheep, a duck, and a rooster. Eighty years later, during the U.S. Civil War, balloons were tethered aloft as aerial observation posts to monitor enemy movements and positions.

Later dreamers built fantastic contraptions that lumbered forward and collapsed in mangled heaps. Still, they climbed from the wreckage to try again. Many eventually gave up, believing powered flight was beyond human capabilities. Others persisted, and none with more determination and scientific precision than brothers Orville and Wilbur Wright.

Through a careful approach, they found ways to control a man-carrying glider in three axes. They designed high-efficiency propellers. They built their own lightweight gasoline engine. And on December 17, 1903, with Orville at the controls, the brothers' fragile wood-and-cloth *Flyer* rose 10 feet from a wooden track laid on the sand in Kitty Hawk, North Carolina, and clattered forward into the brisk sea wind. Twelve seconds and 120 feet later, the world had been changed forever. One witness shouted, "Damned if they ain't flew!" Later, Orville Wright said it best. "We stand at the beginning of a new era—the Age of Flight."

Advances came rapidly. In 1906, flights by Brazil's Alberto Santos-Dumont electrified Paris. In 1909, France's Louis Blériot flew the English Channel. By 1913, a four-engine plane designed by Russian engineer Igor Sikorsky—the first plane to have a glass-enclosed passenger cabin, which included four seats, a table, and a washroom—was flying.

With the beginning of World War I, the airplane quickly evolved from a novel method of transport and observation into a deadly, high-performance weapon. And by the time the war ended in 1918, the Age of Flight was well under way. ///

Riding the wings of the workhorse Boeing 747-400, United grew to global prominence in the late 20th century.

THE EARLY YEARS

I happened to be the man on the spot, but any of the rest of the fellows would have done what I did. —JACK KNIGHT

THE AIRMAIL SERVICE |

AT THE END OF WORLD WAR I, THE UNITED STATES HAD A GREAT FLEET OF AIRPLANES AND HUNDREDS OF TRAINED pilots, but there was little for them to do. Pilots were making meager livings barnstorming across the country, setting down at fairs and carnivals to take a few brave people up for short hops and charging spectators as much as $1 just to see an airplane up close. These wood, wire, and fabric-covered planes, with their open one- and two-seat cockpits, had not been built to carry passengers. And most people remained wary of flying. Charles Lindbergh's mechanic and future United pilot, Harlan "Bud" Gurney, said his mother once told him, "If God had intended man to fly He'd make our bones hollow like the birds'—especially our heads."

Aviation wasn't yet an industry; it was entertainment. But it had nevertheless become obvious that aviation was going to play a vital role in the nation's economic and military future, and the government had to find ways to encourage and support its growth. The answer lay with the Post Office Department. Just as pony express riders had once blazed a trail westward, an airmail service would allow the government to invest in the future of aviation while providing an immediate public benefit. In 1918 the Post Office appropriated $100,000 to open an experimental airmail route between New York City and Washington, DC.

Despite a dubious inauguration of service—one of the pilots got lost, the plane's propeller broke in a rough landing, and the mail had to continue by truck—airmail delivery routes opened rapidly across the nation. By 1920 service extended from New York through Chicago to San Francisco following U.S. Air Mail Route No. 1. That route—known as the Overland Trail to pioneers in covered wagons and engineers on the transcontinental railroad—would eventually become legendary as the Main Line.

Early U.S. Air Mail pilots like Lester Bishop (left) paved the way for commercial aviation in the United States. The insignia above (and left) adorned his de Havilland DH-4 biplane. Bishop flew for a United predecessor.

When the weather cooperated, it took 78 hours of air and rail transport to complete the coast-to-coast journey. Guided mostly by visual contact with landmarks on the ground, brave pilots flew only in daylight hours, transferring the mail they carried to trains or trucks at night. A chain of primitive landing fields was built, but bad weather or darkness often forced airmail pilots to land in pastures. The rare passenger willing to spend hundreds of dollars for a long-distance flight found himself seated in the mail compartment with sacks of mail piled on his feet and lap.

Even after the Post Office lowered the airmail price to the same as regular mail in 1919, airmail remained more of a gimmick than a valuable business tool. By 1920 the airmail experiment had proved to be a financial flop, and Congress began to discuss ending it. If the service were to be saved

U.S. Army Lt. George Boyle and his Curtiss JN4H "Jenny" prepare to inaugurate U.S. Air Mail Service on May 15, 1918, in Washington, DC.

Jack "Skinny" Knight (right, in a DH-4) **_proved the viability of airmail with a daring flight through a snow-filled night from Omaha to Chicago. Later, Knight flew for Boeing Air Transport and United. The gold wings he wore showed that BAT was an official airmail carrier_** (above).

it would have to become more reliable, more efficient, and much faster. The only way to decrease delivery time was to begin flying through the night. With no radios and few beacons on the ground to light the way, night flight increased the risk of what was already a dangerous occupation. Within the first three years of airmail service, 19 of the Post Office's original 40 pilots died in crashes. Even the most courageous pilots wisely chose to land in fields at sunset, rather than risk getting lost in the dark. Just about every aviator had friends who had been killed while flying at night.

But postal officials believed that a land-based lighting system could be installed to guide pilots to the dawn. And on February 22, 1921, they were ready to prove that flying mail through the night was a viable option. Two de Havillands started from each coast. Pilots were positioned across the country to fly different legs of the route, and farmers lit bonfires to mark the way. The two planes heading west from New York encountered foul weather and were forced to land. One of the San Francisco–based planes crashed on takeoff after refueling in Elko, Nevada, and its pilot burned to death. But the last plane, flown by Jack Knight, continued eastward through a snow-filled night.

Knight landed in Omaha only to learn that the ground manager had canceled all flights east due to a blizzard—if the mail was going to get through, he would have to deliver it himself. Although he had never flown the next part of the route before, by using a road map and following railroad tracks, Knight, in his open-cockpit plane, was able to soldier through bitter cold, snow, and fog all the way to Chicago and into history. Knight's mail sacks were transferred to a waiting plane. Reaching New York 33 hours and 20 minutes after departing from San Francisco, the shipment firmly established the practicality of airmail. Almost immediately, Congress granted the Post Office the money to build airports and install beacons to make the service as safe as possible.

By 1925 airmail planes were crisscrossing the country day and night. The railroads were complaining loudly that they could not afford to compete with the government-owned operation. And the Post Office was itself heavily burdened by running a vast airline network. Congress responded by passing the Air Mail Act of February 2, 1925, also called the Kelly Act, "to encourage commercial aviation and to authorize the Postmaster General to contract for the mail service."

The routes staked out by courageous pilots flying flimsy craft were put up for bid. For the first time in history there was real money to be made flying airplanes. The stage was set for commercial aviation. It was a core group of these airmail pilots who got United off the ground. And Jack Knight, who made sure the mail got through, became one of United's legendary captains. ///

Early airmail pilots were a rare breed. E. Hamilton "Ham" Lee, later a United captain, kept this log of his military service in World War I.

Postma...

5.30 A.M
APRIL 6
1926
...NGTON...

Date __April 6___, 192**6**.

...ash. ___,

r mail was dispatched today to Rt.No. **5** , Pasco, W...

...ber of Bags __**6**__ : Weight of Mail xxxxx lbs. xxxxx

: ounce or fraction thereof for this route only $97...

Dispatchin...

bound, today as sh...

was dispatched to RT.No. ___,

SHIP NO.	NAME OF PILOT	MAIL LEFT P.O.*	SHIP
3	Leo Cuddeback	5 37 A M	Leo Cud

Employee at Pasco

...ished by the postmaster.
...ster will file the duplicate co...
...plane for direct conne...
...dispatching cl...

Airmail was an impractical sort of fad and had no place in the serious job of postal transportation. —COLONEL PAUL HENDERSON, U.S. SECOND ASSISTANT POSTMASTER GENERAL, IN 1919

THE ORIGINAL UNITED

ALTHOUGH IN APRIL 1926 LEON "LEE" CUDDEBACK HAD THE GRAND TITLE OF CHIEF PILOT FOR WALTER T. VARNEY'S airline, his world revolved around a small wooden hangar with concrete on half the floor and packed dirt making up the rest. The hangar had been erected not long before as part of a forward-thinking municipal project. City leaders in Boise, Idaho, had ordered the clearing of some city-owned marshland on the Boise River for the creation of a landing strip about 2,000 feet long and 80 feet wide. The construction dispossessed several squatters and resulted in some brief commotion, but things quickly settled down. The city was ready to deliver on its promise to bring Boise into the aviation age.

Of the many Contract Air Mail routes created when Congress put mail-carrying contracts up for bid, none was less appealing than CAM 5. It stretched from Pasco, a small town in eastern Washington state, through Boise, and terminated in Elko, Nevada— a 460-mile run "from nowhere to nowhere" over barren, high desert and tall, cloud-ringed mountains where blizzards reigned throughout the winter.

There was logic behind the difficult route. Pasco was a rail center, roughly equidistant from Portland, Seattle, and Spokane. Mail trains leaving those cities in the evening arrived in Pasco early the next morning. There, mail could be transferred to the contract carrier and then flown through Boise and on to Elko, where it was exchanged with mail destined for the Northwest on Post Office planes flying east and west along the Main Line. Thus a letter posted in Seattle could be delivered to a person in New York City just 47 hours later. Wings were rapidly shrinking the world for ordinary folk.

Leon Cuddeback's paperwork (left) documents his April 6, 1926, flight into history. The official-looking bumper plate (above) identified Varney's mail trucks and was intended to cut down on speeding tickets.

After carefully studying the various routes, Walter T. Varney, a flight school and air taxi operator from San Francisco, decided to make a bid for CAM 5. He concluded that the route was so uninviting that no one else would want it. He was right.

Varney bought six small Swallow biplanes able to accommodate one pilot and 600 pounds of mail each. The airplanes were shipped unassembled from the factory in Wichita to the new Boise Airport, where Cuddeback—a former instructor at the flight school—and his mechanics put them together. They had three of the Swallows airworthy by April 5, 1926, and Cuddeback was in the hangar helping to assemble the fourth late that afternoon when a telegram arrived. It was bad news.

Earlier that day two Varney pilots (one scrunched in the mail pit) had taken off in a Swallow to

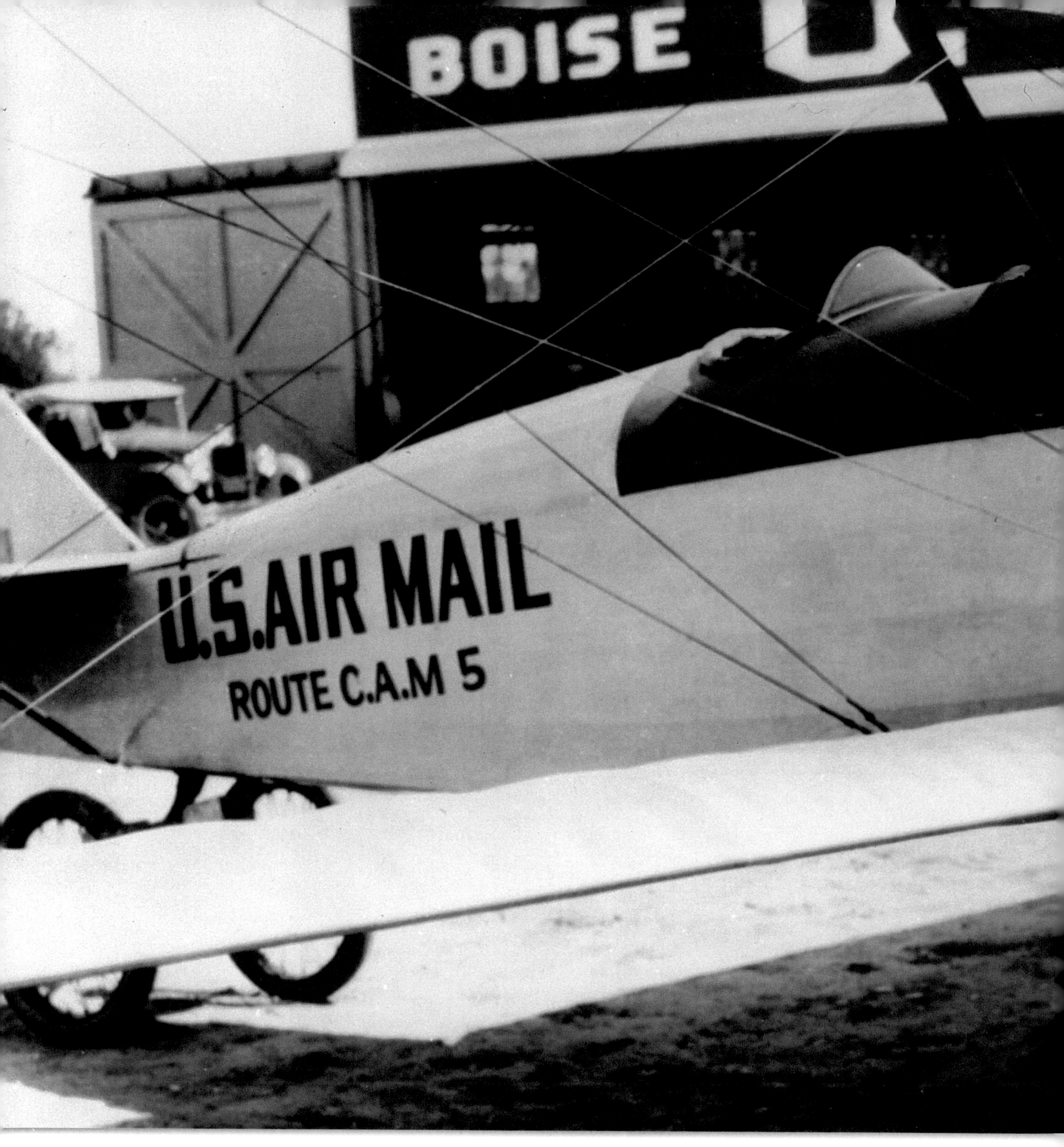
BOISE
U.S. AIR MAIL
ROUTE C.A.M 5

Walter Varney's Chief Pilot Leon "Lee" Cuddeback and one of the six airmail Swallows—this one with the later Wright Whirlwind engine.

On June 1, 1926, Varney received the new Wright Whirlwind J4 engines that would dramatically enhance the performance of the Swallows flying the CAM 5 route. Pilot Leon Cuddeback stands at far right.

deliver the aircraft to Pasco. As it turned out, the Curtiss K6 engine's waterjacket had a tendency to crack at high altitudes, causing water to dilute the gasoline and forcing the pilots down several times. The last forced landing was the worst. The airplane touched down in the desert near Pasco and nosed over, crumpling the Swallow and breaking both pilots' noses. The two airmen were in the hospital when Cuddeback got the word.

The timing could not have been worse. Varney's airmail service was scheduled to begin the following day.

Cuddeback climbed into another Swallow and took off for Pasco, 280 miles to the northwest on the other side of the Blue Mountains. It was dark by the time the 27-year-old airman arrived, and the Swallow was strictly a day plane with no lights inside or out. The field at Pasco was unlighted as well. Fortunately, the people there were resourceful. They lined their cars along the runway's edges, and when they heard Cuddeback's plane, they lit railway flares and turned on their headlights. Cuddeback landed without mishap, refueled the airplane, then ambled off to a hotel.

After waking a few hours later, he downed some coffee and left for the airport. Cuddeback had been so focused on meeting the schedule that he was oblivious to the significance of what he was about to do—pilot the first contract mail flight in the Northwest. The importance was not lost on others, however, and when he reached the airport at 5:30 a.m., Cuddeback was shocked to find reporters, photographers, postal officials, and an estimated 2,500 onlookers there for the takeoff.

Cheers filled the morning air as a stagecoach pulled by a team of six horses came to a halt near the hangar and the riders handed over six sacks of mail containing 9,285 pieces weighing a total of 200 pounds. The mail was loaded aboard and mechanics began hand-pulling the Swallow's prop, but the balky engine refused to crank. Cuddeback became anxious as the 6 a.m. departure time came and went. Finally, after 20 minutes of pulling, the engine caught and Cuddeback roared off for Boise.

Once en route and free of the morning's tension and unexpected spectacle, Cuddeback realized he hadn't used a restroom in Pasco and now the coffee was having its effect. He passed low over the Boise airport at 10 a.m., turned sharply, and set up for an approach. The Swallow's wheels just cleared the telephone wires, and moments later it set down in a perfect three-point landing. Cuddeback stopped halfway down the field and turned east, throwing sand all over youngsters who had followed gleefully behind. As he rumbled up to the company hangar, he was dismayed to see another crowd gathered, as boisterous as the one he'd left in Pasco. More photographers, more officials, more speeches. He loaded two more mail sacks along with a special express package

Throngs cheered Leon Cuddeback's inauguration of contract airmail service. This first flight envelope bears his signature and postmark.

June 6, 1922—U.S. Post Office personnel pose with their de Havilland DH-4 biplanes at Checkerboard Field near Chicago.

It is not necessarily impossible for humans to fly, but it so happens that God did not give them the knowledge of how to do it. It follows therefore that anyone who claims that he can fly must have sought the aid of the devil. To attempt to fly is therefore sinful.

—ROGER BACON, 13TH CENTURY FRANCISCAN FRIAR

FOUNDING FATHERS | 39

THE SKIES WERE CONQUERED BY YOUNG MEN OF GREAT PASSION AND COURAGE WHO RISKED THEIR LIVES EXTENDING the new science and art of aviation while reaching to far horizons. These young flyboys became the rage of a generation, but it took a very different type of pioneer to turn their passion into an industry.

Until the mid-1920s the only profit to be made in aviation was in the manufacture of airplanes and engines. Many people had attempted to start commercial airlines, but few companies survived. There were no regularly scheduled passenger flights, there was little cargo to be carried, few real landing fields had been created, and there was almost no government involvement. That all changed in 1926 with the passage of the Air Commerce Act, championed by Secretary of Commerce Herbert Hoover. These new regulations were modeled on the maritime industry, where the government provided navigation services for ships at sea, but private industry was responsible for all dockside services. Hoover wanted to apply this concept to "ports of air," or "airports," and the civil-aviation industry was born.

Under the act the Department of Commerce took responsibility for establishing safety regulations, licensing pilots and aircraft, and developing a national airways system, as well as promoting aviation in the United States. Three long routes were equipped with radio range beacons, lights to aid navigation, and control towers to supervise traffic in congested areas.

At just about the same time, the United States was falling in love with the airplane. Charles Lindbergh's solo nonstop flight across the Atlantic in 1927 enthralled the nation and the world. Suddenly everyone wanted to get into the cockpit. Aviation was hip. That excitement, combined with the promise of profit through the privatization of mail routes, proved to be a powerful force. Businessmen rushed to buy a piece of the sky. The separate stories of four of those men—Walter Varney, Vern Gorst, Clement Keys, and Bill Boeing—reveal the dramatic struggles that ultimately led to the creation of United Airlines.

WALTER VARNEY / Walter T. Varney spent World War I teaching future military aviators to fly at March Field in Riverside, California. Once the war ended, he continued as a flight instructor by opening Varney Flying School near San Francisco. An enthusiastic aviation promoter, Varney began using his open-cockpit trainers as air taxis, shuttling adventurous passengers back and forth across San Francisco Bay.

In this 1926 photo (left), a Varney pilot shows the lighter side of being an airmail pioneer. While some of the equipment was needed, including the headgear (above), even an emergency landing in remote terrain rarely required a pigeon.

Building on that experience, Varney then began a scheduled air express service, flying a triangular route between San Francisco, Modesto, and Stockton in California's San Joaquin Valley. Varney used his instructors and most promising students as pilots on the route, helping them gain valuable experience while keeping his operating costs low. This primitive passenger service was a success.

In 1926 Varney's venture shifted to contract airmail carrier when his successful bid netted CAM 5 from Pasco, Washington, through Boise, Idaho, and on to Elko, Nevada. Although the venture initially lost money, that changed after the Post Office increased the rate and extended the line to Seattle, Portland, and Salt Lake City. Within a few years, the Varney route was transporting $1 million worth of mail annually. Varney reached for more, bidding on airmail routes all over the country and even Mexico, but he came away empty-handed.

Thoroughly enjoying the high life of an airline mogul, Varney traveled extensively and expensively. Life was good, but money was nevertheless tight. So, when Bill Boeing offered to buy him out in 1930, he jumped at the offer.

A newly minted millionaire, Varney sought to extend his aviation fortune. He bought a fleet of fast Lockheed Vega monoplanes and in 1934 launched Varney Speed Lines, with service in California and the Rockies. The venture proved to be a money loser. Varney went broke and ceded control to his partner. In the end, the struggling carrier survived to become Continental Airlines.

His money gone, Varney returned to the cockpit as a test pilot. Later he became a sand-and-gravel-truck operator, steering heavy rigs over the mountains he'd conquered only a short time before with fabric, wood, and flying wires.

VERN GORST / Vern Gorst was a man involved in movement. He was born in the United States' 100th anniversary year of 1876, and his parents proudly named him Vern Centennial Gorst. Lured by the wide-open West, the family sold its Minnesota lumber and grist mills in 1888 and moved to Washington state. Even then an outdoorsman, Vern fell in love with his new home, its bounty of fish and game, and the ready access to woodlands and open water. He loved the adventure of the place and embraced that spirit throughout his life.

At 20, Gorst headed north to Alaska to seek his fortune panning for gold in the Yukon and made money backpacking supplies over the Chilcoot Pass at $1 per pound.

Returning to Washington, he continued in the transportation business in Seattle, this time carrying passengers and goods in boats between Port Orchard and the Bremerton Navy Yard. By 1910 he was operating a local bus line, and soon thereafter he joined with others in offering bus service up and down the West Coast.

In 1915 Gorst set off on an entirely new adventure by taking flying lessons and then purchasing a pontoon-equipped biplane built by Glenn L. Martin. Unfortunately, it wasn't long before the aircraft—a fabric-and-wire contraption known as a Flying Birdcage—was destroyed in an accident. Perennially short of money, Gorst didn't have the resources to rebuild the machine, so his newfound passion for aviation would have to wait.

The circumstances were right for rekindling the flame in 1925. It was then that Gorst learned the Post Office was about to turn over airmail routes to private companies. He went to his fellow bus operators and raised enough money to conduct an aerial survey of the proposed coastal routes. Satisfied that mail planes could operate safely over the hazardous terrain,

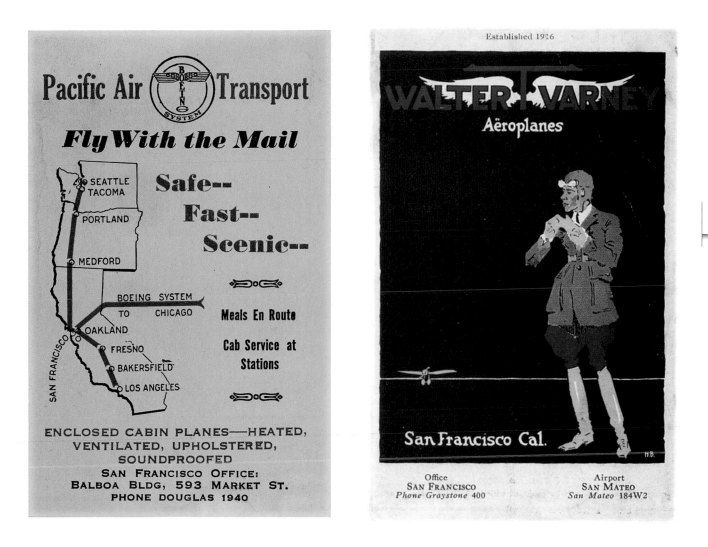

Gorst began earnestly searching for capital, trading stock in his new company for money and services.

Gorst's bid to carry mail between Los Angeles, San Francisco, Portland, and Seattle won the competition, and Pacific Air Transport (PAT)—cash-strapped but rich in potential—was on its way. The airline began scheduled operations in September 1926 with a ragtag collection of World War I biplanes. Three PAT pilots were killed in crashes that unusually severe first winter. Mail revenue failed to cover expenses. The following March, Gorst's never-ending money hunt led him to the Wells Fargo Bank in San Francisco and a meeting with an eager young assistant vice president named William "Pat" Patterson, who agreed to lend him $5,000. But by 1928, PAT's fortunes had not much improved and Gorst readily accepted a $94,000 buyout by Boeing.

Gorst went on to operate flying services in Alaska and then in Seattle for several years, but he eventually left aviation and returned to the bus business. He raised trout and catfish commercially, continued to hunt and fish and occasionally tried panning for gold throughout the West. He remained an active pilot until right before his death in Portland in 1953.

CLEMENT KEYS / Born in Ontario, Canada, in 1876, Clement Melville Keys immigrated to the United States when he was 25. There, with a background in finance, he worked as a reporter and railroad news editor at *The Wall Street Journal*. In 1911, he founded

Founding fathers: (Clockwise from upper right) **Bill Boeing** (R)**; Walter Varney; Clement Keys** (R) **with Lindbergh; Vern Gorst** (L)**.**

Like early steamship lines and railroads, the airlines used stickers to advertise (right)*. Travelers put them on suitcases, where they became status symbols. These, and the penny postcards on pages 46 and 47, are today prized by collectors of airline memorabilia.*

C.M. Keys and Company, an investment counseling firm and bond dealer. Keys was one of the first entrepreneurs to recognize the promise of aviation, and his success on Wall Street gave him the fiscal freedom to join the financially troubled Curtiss Aeroplane & Motor Company, an airplane manufacturer, as an unsalaried vice president in 1916. Four years later he bought the company.

When the government announced in 1925 that it was soliciting bids on its airmail routes, Keys and investors in Chicago and Detroit raised more than $2 million and founded National Air Transport (NAT). The airline eventually bid for and won exclusive rights to the mail route between Chicago and Dallas and then, in 1927, added the vitally important New York–Chicago route. In Chicago, NAT connected with Boeing Air Transport (BAT) and its Chicago–San Francisco service, establishing the nation's first commercial coast-to-coast route.

Keys invested heavily in all aspects of aviation. At one time he operated 26 different companies, including NAT, China Airways, and the first regularly scheduled air-rail transcontinental passenger service, Transcontinental Air Transport (TAT). Keys based his success on efficient, cost-conscious ground operations, believing that "Ten percent of aviation is in the air and 90 percent is on the ground."

The U.S. aviation industry was growing rapidly; in 1926 only 5,800 paying customers traveled by air, but within four years that number grew to 173,000. TAT promoted itself as The Lindbergh Line, because Keys had hired the Lone Eagle as technical advisor for the then-incredible annual salary of $10,000 plus stock options. The carrier promised to transport passengers in great comfort from coast to coast in only two days by linking up with the railroads. But weather cancelled so many flights that pilots joked that TAT really stood for "Take a Train." As it turned out, most people preferred to do just that rather than pay TAT's princely ticket price of $480. The carrier lost $2.7 million in 18 months.

Keys' holding company was able to absorb TAT's losses until the Depression ended a decade of opulence. A fight for survival followed, leading to numerous mergers and takeovers. It was widely believed that the key to financial success was control of a single coast-to-coast route. While Keys was moving westward, Boeing and his partners were looking to the East and setting their sights on NAT. The two airlines met in Chicago and fed passengers into each other's systems. But Keys firmly rejected that offer and a corporate takeover battle ensued. In 1930, Boeing's group prevailed. That same year Boeing's United Aircraft & Transport Corporation (UATC) acquired NAT to form the nation's first coast-to-coast airline. In 1934, UATC was dissolved and United Air Lines Transport Corporation was formed as owner and operator of BAT, NAT, PAT, and Varney Air Lines. The names of the four predecessor airlines were dropped and replaced with United Air Lines.

His aviation empire crumbling, Keys eventually lost control of TAT, which grew to become Trans World Airlines. Finally, in 1932, citing his ill health, Clement Keys discarded his aviation companies. One of the legendary settlers of the skies was done.

BILL BOEING / His German immigrant father had made a fortune in Minnesota timber and iron ore. Eager to further that tradition, 22-year-old William E. Boeing left Yale's Sheffield School of Science after his junior year and headed West to the forests of Washington state. The year was 1903. Trading forest lands around Grays Harbor, he beat the high-risk odds and cyclical nature of the timber business and, within a few years, had earned his own fortune.

Despite a professorial look and quiet manner, Boeing was an adventurer in business and recreation. Perhaps inevitably he became interested in the newly invented airplane, and in 1914 he and Commander G. Conrad Westervelt, a friend and Naval engineer, took an excursion hop from Seattle's Lake Washington in a Curtiss biplane. Westervelt later wrote that he "could never find any definite answer as to why [the wood and fabric conveyance] held together."

Boeing thought he and Westervelt could produce something better. So he charged his friend to design a more substantial float-plane while he departed to take piloting lessons in Los Angeles from aviation pioneer Glenn Martin. The resulting aircraft—completed after the Navy reassigned Westervelt to a post in the East—was the B&W, the first of what was to become a steady stream of ever more capable flying machines produced by Boeing's plant in Seattle.

With the arrival of World War I, the little Boeing factory prospered, building 50 trainers for the U.S. Navy, the company's first production order. But once hostilities ended, military orders ceased and the civilian market was flooded with surplus flying machines. Business became so slim that at one point Boeing resorted to making wooden dressers, nightstands, beds, and boats to survive.

But eventually business turned again, and key executives urged Boeing to bid on the U.S. Post Office contract for flying airmail daily between San Francisco and Chicago, the longest route in the nationwide system. He won, and Boeing Air Transport began service in 1927. In its first year, BAT carried 837,211 pounds of mail, 149,000 pounds of express packages, and 1,863 intrepid passengers.

Charles Lindbergh's transatlantic solo flight that same year spurred tremendous interest in the business of aviation. Helping lead a surge in acquisitions, Bill Boeing began merging with and acquiring other airmail and passenger carriers in 1929. Accordingly he renamed the company United Aircraft & Transport Corporation and served as its chairman and a principal stockholder. With the acquisition of National Air Transport in 1930, UATC became the most formidable business entity in American aviation.

When government intervention forced the dissolution of his company in 1934, Boeing, disheartened, disillusioned, but wealthy, resigned as chairman, sold his stock, and withdrew from aviation entirely. He was 53. Thereafter Bill Boeing led a life of leisure—raising horses and cattle, fishing, and sailing. He died of a heart attack aboard his yacht *Taconite* in 1956. ///

FLY

LOWER Summer Rates

SAN FRANCISCO
LOS ANGELES
SAN DIEGO

SEATTLE

1½ Hrs.

PORTLAND

5½ Hrs.

SAN FRANCISCO

3 Hrs.

LOS ANGELES

1 Hr.

SAN DIEGO

These Advantages cost no more

1 Pacific Coast's Pioneer Air Mail-Passenger Line.

2 5 years and 4 million miles experience on this route.

3 Latest types tri-motored transports.

4 Three 450 H. P. Wasp motors.

5 Two transport pilots on each tri-motored plane.

6 Two-way radio telephone.

7 Stewardess Service.

NEW LOW RATES BETWEEN:

San Francisco and Los Angeles......$18.95
San Francisco and San Diego........... 22.95
Los Angeles and San Diego............. 4.95

NEW RATE TO NEW YORK, $200.00
CHICAGO, $150.00.

FOR RESERVATIONS OR INFORMATION:

San Francisco, 320 Geary St.____DOuglas 1940
Los Angeles, 749 So. Hill St.____TRinity 3434
San Diego, Lindbergh Field_____Hillcrest 4437

"Air Transportation at Its Best"
Frequent Services Each Way DAILY

[*Above Rates also apply via Trans-*
continental and Western Air, Inc.]

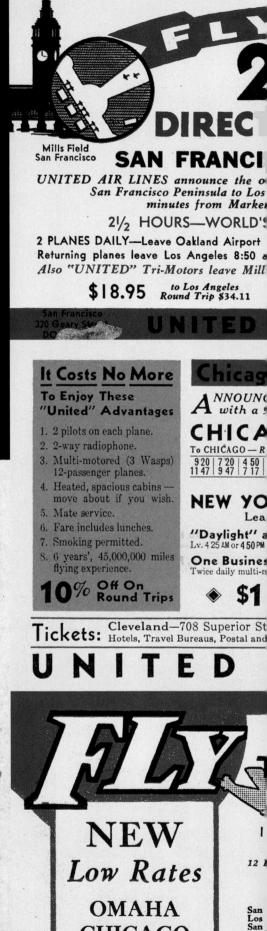

FLY

2 DIRECT

Mills Field
San Francisco

SAN FRANCI

UNITED AIR LINES announce the o
San Francisco Peninsula to Los
minutes from Marke

2½ HOURS—WORLD'S

2 PLANES DAILY—Leave Oakland Airport
Returning planes leave Los Angeles 8:50 a
Also "UNITED" Tri-Motors leave Mill

$18.95   to Los Angeles
Round Trip $34.11

San Francisco
320 Geary St
DO

UNITED

It Costs No More
To Enjoy These
"United" Advantages

1. 2 pilots on each plane.
2. 2-way radiophone.
3. Multi-motored (3 Wasps) 12-passenger planes.
4. Heated, spacious cabins — move about if you wish.
5. Mate service.
6. Fare includes lunches.
7. Smoking permitted.
8. 6 years', 45,000,000 miles flying experience.

10% Off On Round Trips

Chica

A NNOUNC
with a

CHICA

To CHICAGO—R

| 9 20 | 7 20 | 4 50 |
| 11 47 | 9 47 | 7 17 |

NEW YO
Lea

"Daylight" a
Lv. 4 25 AM or 4 50 PM

One Busines
Twice daily multi-m

$1

Tickets: Cleveland—708 Superior St
Hotels, Travel Bureaus, Postal and

UNITED

FLY

NEW
Low Rates

OMAHA
CHICAGO

12

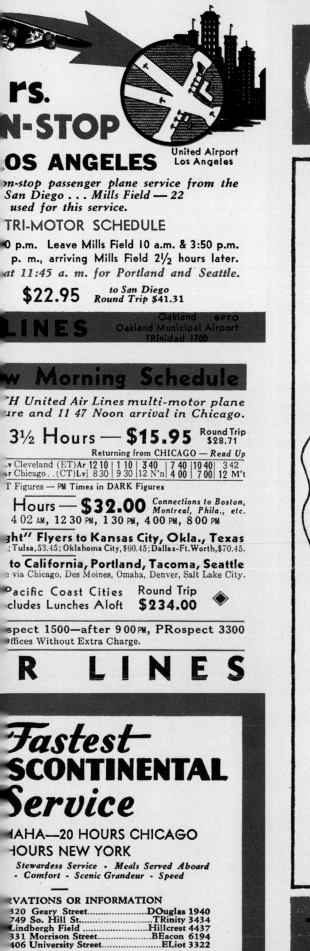

Passenger traffic has been booming at this station recently.
One day we sold three roundtrips to Portland.
–JUNE 1933 UNITED REPORT FROM BOISE STATION

BECOMING UNITED | 49

WILLIAM BOEING WON THE SAN FRANCISCO–CHICAGO AIRMAIL CONTRACT IN 1927 BY OFFERING TO FLY THE MAIL for $1.50 a pound for the first 1,000 miles and 15 cents a pound for each additional 100 miles. That meant he was willing to carry the mail halfway across the nation for less than the Post Office was paying to send it from New York to Boston. The bid was so low that skeptical postal officials insisted Boeing post an $800,000 bond to guarantee operations. Competitors were certain he would fail; it was simply a question of how quickly. But Boeing had based his bid upon the success of a reconfigured Boeing aircraft, the Model 40A. The aircraft would feature an open cockpit, a small two-seat passenger cabin, and, most important, the new Pratt & Whitney Wasp engine.

Prior to the 40A, most mail planes were fitted with heavy, water-cooled engines with in-line cylinders. By contrast, the new Wasp had cylinders arranged radially around a central hub, allowing them to be cooled by the air as it rushed by, and thus it had no radiator, plumbing, or coolant. The 40A would exchange that weight for revenue-producing mail, cargo, and passengers. Because the Wasp-powered aircraft carried twice the payload of any other mail plane, the newly created Boeing Air Transport made money from its very first day of operations in 1927.

Boeing believed that to truly succeed his line had to grow. And so in 1928, he jumped at the chance to add Pacific Air Transport (PAT) to his operation. PAT served the Los Angeles-Seattle route and points in between.

Boeing, a quiet, private man, had few cronies. But one of those pals was Frederick Brant Rentschler, the energetic head of Pratt

The Boeing 40A (left) carried twice the payload of any other mail plane and made a giant, though dubious, leap in luxury—a passenger cabin for two behind the engine. Boeing Air Transport's first schedule holder from 1929 (above).

& Whitney and the man who had taken control of that former machine-tool company with the express intent of developing the Wasp. Rentschler's belief in the engine was well placed; it proved to be a tremendous success.

During a conversation with Boeing in late 1928, Rentschler made a startling proposition, suggesting they join their companies. The concept of an all-encompassing aviation concern that manufactured engines and airframes and then operated the products for profit immediately appealed to Boeing. One witness to the exchange was Chance Vought, a pioneering pilot whose eponymous company specialized in building two-seat fighters and observation aircraft for the Army and Navy. Vought said he liked the idea, too, and wanted to be part of the new company.

Timetables for United and predecessor airlines in the late 1920s and early 1930s (following pages) *did double duty as promotional material. The United Air Lines office in Seattle, Washington* (right) *in 1931. Window ads urged people to "be modern" and fly.*

When the combined company, United Aircraft & Transport Corporation (UATC), came to life on February 1, 1929, its manufacturing subsidiaries were Boeing Airplane Co., Pratt & Whitney Engine, Chance Vought, Hamilton Standard Propeller Co., Sikorsky Aircraft Co. (which then made flying boats), light-plane builder Stearman Aircraft Co., and Northrop Aircraft Co. Its airlines were Boeing Air Transport (BAT) and Pacific Air Transport (PAT). An aviation colossus from the outset, UATC expanded quickly and, within the year, added Stout Air Services, a Midwestern passenger carrier. But the prize acquisitions were yet to come.

UATC wanted to extend its airmail and passenger service beyond Chicago and Cleveland all the way to New York. To accomplish that, United Aircraft President Frederick Rentschler proposed merging with National Air Transport (NAT), which held the New York–Chicago mail contract. On March 31, 1930, NAT became a UATC subsidiary. With that, the first transcontinental airline was formed. Three months later, UATC acquired Varney Air Lines, extending its reach throughout the Northwest.

In its first annual report, United Aircraft quite rightly said that the corporation "occupies a unique and possibly the strongest position in the aeronautical field of any company in the world." The future looked bright, and it was—although short-lived. The Great Depression took hold across the land, and big business was widely blamed for creating it. Franklin Roosevelt became president and assumed the mandate to resolve the economic crisis by whatever means necessary.

It was in this climate that Congress began investigating the methods used by the Post Office to award airmail contracts. During the hearings in Washington, DC, it was revealed that the former postmaster general had given preferential treatment to the largest carriers in awarding certain contracts. Roosevelt reacted with vengeance. In February 1934, all airmail contracts were cancelled, including those of UATC's carriers, despite the fact that none of them was among the tainted awards. Roosevelt simultaneously assigned the Army Air Corps to carry the mail, a decision that proved disastrous.

The public outcry included critical words from humorist Will Rogers: "What's all the hundreds of airplane pilots and the hundreds of people who make an honest living in the airplane business going to do? It's like finding a crooked railroad president, then stopping all of the trains."

The Army planes proved to be ill-equipped and their pilots unprepared for flying long distances in foul weather and at night. By the end of the first week, five Army pilots had died in crashes. Seven more perished in the following month. Public disapproval was so vocal that Roosevelt reversed his decision and put the mail routes up for bid again.

By then UATC had lost more than $850,000. And the news got worse. Congress passed legislation prohibiting any connection between aviation-related manufacturing companies and airlines. United Aircraft & Transport Corporation, the country's first aeronautical powerhouse, was suddenly an illegal entity and had to disassemble itself.

Accordingly, Boeing and Stearman departed to build airplanes. The Eastern manufacturing subsidiaries, including Pratt & Whitney, Sikorsky, Chance Vought, Northrop, and Hamilton Standard, continued as UATC. And on July 20, 1934, a new holding company was formed—United Air Lines Transport Corporation. The responsibility for carrying the mail and passengers along the Main Line fell to a newly independent part of the holding company called United Air Lines. ⫻

CHICAGO OMAHA SALT LAKE CITY
RENO OAKLAND **SAN FRANCISCO**
SEATTLE TACOMA PORTLAND
OAKLAND SAN FRANCISCO LOS ANGELES **SAN DIEGO**

by **AIR**
BOEING SYSTEM

"Fly with the BOEING SYSTEM *AirMail"*

Division of United Aircraft and Transport Corp.

UNITED AIR LINES

30 MILLION MILES FLYING EXPERIENCE

**NEW YORK
CHICAGO
PACIFIC COAST
KANSAS CITY
DALLAS**

UNITED AIR LINES

Air Transportation at Its Best

Copyright 1931, United Air Lines, Inc.

BOEING AIR TRANSPORT
NATIONAL AIR TRANSPORT
PACIFIC AIR TRANSPORT
VARNEY AIR LINES

UNITED AIR LINES

SUBSIDIARY OF UNITED AIRCRAFT & TRANSPORT CORP.

EFFECTIVE JULY 15, 1931

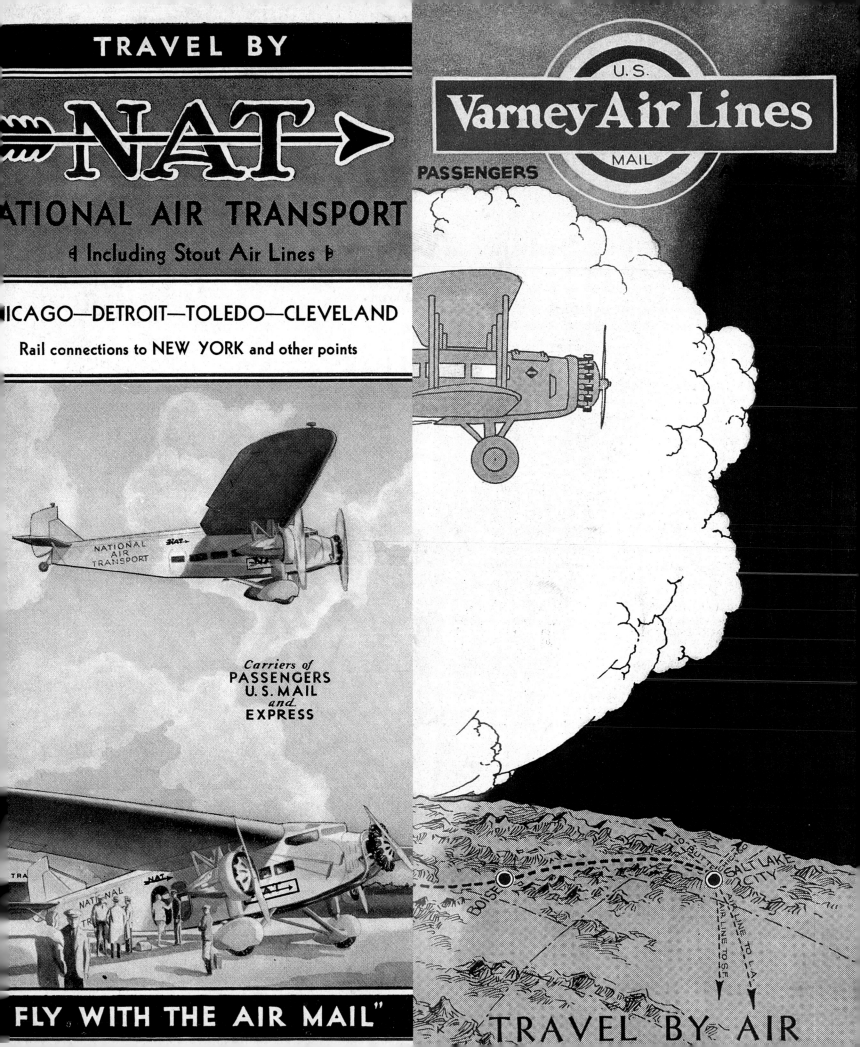

TRAVEL BY

NAT →

NATIONAL AIR TRANSPORT

◄ Including Stout Air Lines ►

CHICAGO—DETROIT—TOLEDO—CLEVELAND

Rail connections to NEW YORK and other points

Carriers of
PASSENGERS
U. S. MAIL
and
EXPRESS

"FLY WITH THE AIR MAIL"

PASSENGERS

Varney Air Lines

U.S. MAIL

TRAVEL BY AIR

Some of our competitors think we took over Capital Airlines to make United the biggest airline in the country ... But that isn't why we took over Capital. We don't particularly care about running the largest airline. We would rather run the best.

—W. A. PATTERSON

PAT PATTERSON | 55

IN 1929, WHEN 29-YEAR-OLD WILLIAM ALLAN PATTERSON GAVE UP HIS SECURE POSITION AT WELLS FARGO BANK TO join Boeing Airplane Co. and Boeing Air Transport as assistant to President Philip Johnson, there were only about 25,000 miles of airways in the United States, and all passenger airlines combined carried fewer than one million passengers annually. When "Pat" Patterson retired as chairman/CEO of United Airlines 32 years later after turning United into the largest passenger carrier in the free world, the airline annually carried more than 18 million passengers into the skies he had helped make so friendly.

Few major corporations have been so completely shaped by the wisdom and direction of a single person as United Airlines. Almost from its very beginning, United was unmistakably the creation of Pat Patterson. Born in 1899 in Hawai'i, where his father managed a sugar plantation, Patterson sailed to the mainland after his father's death, beginning his career at Wells Fargo in 1915 as a 15-year-old office boy. Twelve years later, the newly promoted assistant vice president was approached by Vern Gorst, the president of floundering Pacific Air Transport. Gorst needed a $5,000 loan to keep his airline in business. At that time, *airline* and *business* were two words that did not go well together, but Patterson long had been fascinated by flying machines. Unlike most people, he'd actually flown in an airplane, paying $5—two weeks' salary—in 1919 for the thrill of a 20-minute flight over San Francisco harbor.

This was Patterson's first new account, and to make sure the bank got its money back he began spending time with Gorst at the airline's facilities. Even after the loan was paid back Patterson remained involved in PAT's business affairs. When PAT needed to purchase the latest Boeing model to stay in business, Patterson flew with Gorst to Seattle and convinced William Boeing and

Pat Patterson was president of United Air Lines from 1934–1963 and then chairman/CEO until retirement in 1966. He set the strategy that transformed United from a collection of small airlines into one of the world's largest carriers.

Philip Johnson, president of Boeing Air Transport (BAT), to buy all of PAT's outstanding stock. Gorst made a substantial profit and PAT became part of Boeing Air Transport. More important, within a few months so did Patterson, who was hired in 1929 to assist Johnson.

A year and a half after leaving the bank, Patterson had become executive vice president and general manager. As BAT continued to acquire smaller airlines, Patterson soon found himself in Chicago running America's largest and most successful airline company, having moved the executive offices there from Seattle in 1931.

In the early 1930s, one of the first major decisions he made changed the face of the airline industry. Accepting the suggestion of San Francisco traffic manager Steve Stimpson, Patterson approved the

Patterson personified United. He appeared on Time's April 21, 1947, issue, steering the airline from above. Like the men who piloted Mainliners and wore the captain's buttons on page 55, Patterson guided United to global prominence.

hiring of eight young nurses to care for the needs of passengers, creating a new profession for women—the "stewardess."

The list of other innovations pioneered by United while Patterson was at the helm covers just about every area of the industry. United opened commercial aviation's first flight kitchen and its first research laboratory. It was the first airline to fly passengers coast to coast on regular schedules and long distances at night; it was the first to use two-way radios, in-flight telephones, and television; it pioneered promotional flights like "take your wife free," "executive men only," and the famed "Nurseryliner" for mothers traveling with young children.

Patterson became president of United Air Lines in 1934 when Johnson was forced to leave the company during the dispute with the government about the distribution of airmail routes. Soon after taking charge, Patterson established the priorities by which he would run the airline for the rest of his career. Called The Rule of Five, they were, in order of importance, safety, passenger comfort, dependability, honesty, and sincerity.

Patterson believed completely that United's single biggest asset was its employees. He did everything possible to encourage employee participation in creating airline policy. "When our company was smaller," he once remembered, "we had no industrial relations experience. We had to get our ideas from our employees. I spent up to a third of my time out along the line listening at all hours of the day and night to the people who did the airline's work. When that became impossible because of the number of United employees, I met with larger groups in the major centers along our system. I wanted to get their viewpoint and answer their questions firsthand. I believe that every employee is entitled to a candid answer to any question he wants to ask me about our business.

"I always considered it a tribute, one that I cherish highly, that people on all levels of our business have called me by my first name. When they said, 'Hello, Pat,' I always felt good." In return, Patterson's ability to remember employees by name was legendary throughout the company.

But Patterson never forgot that he was running a business—"a 600-mile-an-hour industry," as he referred to it—and that meant answering to stockholders and producing profits. Responding to someone who questioned the validity of making decisions based on financial return, he wrote, "Would we have a better air transportation system if there were no profits? Would it be better if the airlines just made a little profit, enough to keep them alive, but feeble? Or is the industry entitled to a healthy profit that will permit it to pay good wages and ample dividends, to liquidate debts expeditiously and accumulate financial strength for further advances? Coast-to-coast air travel became possible in 1927 but it called for a strong back, an adventurous spirit, and $400 to pay the fare for the trip that took 32 hours—at least on paper—with no inflight movies to pass the time. Today you can fly a jetliner from one coast to the other at a fare 63 percent lower than in 1927 and at a speed increase of over 500 percent . . . Now I ask, could this advance, unparalleled in the history of transportation or any other industry, have been made without profit?"

When Patterson retired in 1966, Gardner Cowles, a member of the board of directors, offered a resolution, which read in part, "The eyes of Pat Patterson have been upon the stars, while his feet remained firmly planted on the ground ..." Like Eddie Rickenbacker, C.R. Smith, and Juan Trippe, Pat Patterson was one of the legendary visionaries who created modern air transport.

TIME

THE WEEKLY NEWSMAGAZINE

Artzybasheff

UNITED'S PATTERSON

Why be first?

(Business)

MISS MIER, R. N.

The plane ran out of gas and had to make an emergency landing in a wheat field. People from the surrounding area came in wagons and on horseback to see the plane. They'd never seen an aircraft before, and they wanted to touch it and to touch me. One of them called me "the angel from the sky."

—Inez Keller Fuite, one of United's Original Eight stewardesses

THEY ALSO SERVE

In 1930, a young woman named Ellen Church walked into Steve Stimpson's office at Boeing Air Transport in San Francisco and helped create a new profession for women that would change the face of air travel. Eight years earlier, Britain's Daimler Airways hired the world's first male cabin attendants. These cabin boys, as they were called, served no refreshments, but their presence added a comfortable formality to the flight. Other airlines followed. Four years later, Stout Air Services, which eventually was acquired by United Aircraft & Transport Corporation, hired America's first inflight service personnel—young men officially known as aerial couriers. In 1929 Pan American Airways hired "alert and good-looking" young men as stewards. But until 1930, all airline cabin attendants were male. Few people believed women were suitable for work in aviation. It was a man's world—dirty, daring, and sometimes dangerous.

Stimpson had previously worked for a steamship line and knew from experience how much passengers relied on stewards. So as a way to promote Boeing's service, he suggested and received permission to hire several stewards to serve passengers. He had already hired three men when Ellen Church walked into his office and suggested he instead hire female nurses to do the job. Although Boeing managers initially turned down the idea, it was eventually approved by Pat Patterson. A new profession had been born that would become synonymous with glamour and world travel.

But it didn't begin that way. Stimpson hired eight registered nurses, primarily because "they are not given to flightiness—I mean, in the head. The average graduate nurse is a girl with some horse sense and is very practical and has seen enough of men to not be inclined to chase them around the block at every opportunity." These "sky girls," as they were being called by some, were paid $125 a month to fly a minimum of 100 hours.

Although there was no formal training, Ellen Church and Steve Stimpson developed a manual of do's and don'ts. Some of the items covered included: "A ready smile is essential" and "A rigid military salute will be rendered the captain and copilot as they come aboard."

In addition to serving meals, there were many other tasks to be performed by these stewardesses—the job title bestowed "until a more suitable name can be found," wrote Church. Their jobs included duties such as welcoming passengers, punching their tickets and giving refunds when necessary at each stop, weighing the passengers and their baggage (airplane performance was poor so weight was

When United "created" stewardesses, they were nurses, like the one at left, circa 1930. Some placed nameplates in the cabin (above). Ultimately, stewardesses became icons of the Aviation Age (preceding pages).

The Original Eight stewardesses (right; Ellen Church 3rd from left) *were paid $125 for 100 hours of flying monthly. Duties included serving meals and even knocking down fences so planes could take off again after being forced down by weather.*

62

critical), loading and unloading that baggage, making sure the wicker seats were bolted down, dusting the windowsills, carrying buckets of fuel to the plane when necessary, and swatting flies in the cabin. Stewardesses also made sure the passengers did not throw lighted cigarettes out the windows or mistakenly open the emergency exit door when they intended to use the "blue room," the lavatory.

Stewardesses adjusted the clocks and altimeters in the cabin, handed out chewing gum, blankets, ammonia capsules, and slippers on night flights, cleaned passengers' shoes, swept the floor, and carried a railroad timetable in case connections had to be made. If a plane was forced to land in a farmer's field, the stewardess might help knock down fences and clear the way so the plane could take off safely. Once finished for the night, she occasionally would help push the airplane into its hangar before heading home.

Initially the Original Eight received quite a bit of resistance from pilots; they felt so strongly that women did not belong on airplanes that for several flights they refused to speak to them. Pilots' wives were unhappy about the prospect of attractive single women traveling with their husbands and even started a letter-writing campaign to persuade Boeing to end the experiment. But the pilots were quickly won over by the dedication and professionalism of the new stewardesses.

Passengers needed little convincing; they loved the stewardess concept. After three months, passenger traffic had surged and some businessmen were even making reservations to fly with specific stewardesses. Stimpson's experiment was a success, and Boeing hired an additional 20 sky girls. Within a year, most major U.S. airlines were hiring women to serve passengers inflight.

Boeing had very strict hiring policies. Applicants had to be under 25 years old, no more than 5 feet 4 inches tall, and weigh no more than 115 pounds. They had to be registered nurses. And perhaps strictest of all, the stewardess applicants had to be single to get the job.

Stimpson and Church designed the first stewardess uniform, which consisted of a dark green wool cape lined with gray, a double-breasted suit jacket worn over a white roundneck blouse, a calf-length skirt with front pleats, and black oxfords with sensible heels. While in flight, the stewardesses donned their nurses caps and smocks.

United executives soon realized that "the 'sky girls' were the airline's best contact with the flying public." Turnover remained high due to the no-marriage rule, and prior to the beginning of World War II, the average length of employment for a stewardess was slightly more than one year.

To replace departing stewardesses, United instituted a very brief training program, although stewardess Mary O'Connor remembers being told, "No one from the highest officials down could be sure what was included in the stewardesses' duties." But in 1936, as the legendary DC-3 went online, United opened the first stewardess training center in Cheyenne, Wyoming. During the training courses, young women were taught how to take tickets, serve hot meals, and perform safety procedures—as well as take the name and address of every passenger so the airline could send letters of apology should there be a problem during the flight.

In 1942, stewardesses, whose nursing training was desperately needed by the military, went to war along with the rest of the airline. In addition to the many women who came out of retirement to serve, active stewardesses worked on air evacuation

missions in Europe and Africa. On the home front, planes were flying filled to official capacity. To replenish the depleted stewardess ranks, United began accepting young women with a minimum of two years of college or a year of college combined with a year of business experience. The airline did not relax the rule about being unmarried, and stewardesses continued to put in long hours for low pay, working under difficult conditions. One woman remembers sleeping on bunk beds set up in hangars.

In 1945, the first stewardess union was formed at United and, beginning in December of that year, working conditions were negotiated by the union. Being a stewardess had long been a profession, but now stewardesses were becoming professionals.

And glamorous professionals at that. The media created the image of stewardesses—lovely young women flying all over the newly peaceful world leading adventurous, romantic lives. And it was pretty much true. Like all airlines, United was using attractive women to attract business. During hiring interviews, it was not unusual for an applicant to be asked to lift her skirt to allow the interviewer to see her legs. The uniform was a sleek tailored suit with gloves, hat, and navy-and-white spectator shoes. Inflight hairstyles, clothing, and makeup had to be perfect. Girdles were required, and stocking seams had to be straight.

During the war, the size of the airline doubled to almost 8,000 employees, and for the first time women began working in many aspects of the aviation industry. In the postwar years, as the planes got larger and carried more passengers on longer flights, the responsibilities of stewardesses also changed. They had to learn and practice increasingly numerous safety procedures, manage paperwork, and deal with a great variety of human problems. In essence, they were becoming inflight ambassadors. As a 1953 ad explained, United's stewardesses had "good sense, good humor, fine character, a genuine liking for people and an ability to serve them with tact and understanding." And they were still required to maintain a neat and well-groomed appearance.

Two decades after the first stewardesses were hired, United began hiring male stewards. The "Original Eight" men began working in 1950 only on flights between the Mainland and Hawai'i. The significant difference in requirements was that men were permitted to be married.

While the image was glamorous, often the job was not. For both stewards and stewardesses, schedules changed monthly, and those with less seniority "stood reserve," meaning they had to remain mostly at home in case they were needed and be ready to leave on a trip within hours. But the job requirements were eased slightly—maximum height was raised to 5 feet 8 inches and weight to 132 pounds.

"Now she's ready to serve you in the Mainliner manner," promised a 1953 ad (right). *Stewardesses wore silver wings* (above) *from 1937 to 1951. The campy 1968 photo of Hollywood-designed uniforms* (following pages) *epitomized the media image of stewardesses as single, attractive, and fun-loving.*

The Jet Age brought an entirely new fleet of planes to United. Gradually the old prop planes were replaced. The 1964 Civil Rights Act brought changes to the airplane cabin attendant job that turned a short-term adventure into a potential career. By the late 1960s, the no-marriage rule was eliminated and married stewardesses could take pregnancy leave. Height and weight restrictions were also eased and, by the late 1970s, pregnant stewardesses could continue to fly.

Even the uniform was changed from the restrictive form-fitting suits to looser, more casual clothing, making it more comfortable to work. And with all these came a name change. For many years people had been searching for a better name for the profession, and everything from "air hostess" to "airess" had been considered. In 1975 United and the Association of Flight Attendants representing stewards and stewardesses negotiated to change the titles of "stewardess" and "steward" to the more professional and gender-neutral description of "flight attendant." By the end of the decade, about half of United's 8,700 flight attendants were married, and their average age was 31.

As United expanded to become one of the world's largest airlines, more flight attendants were hired. By the end of the 20th century, Ellen Church's Original Eight had grown to more than 25,000 men and women serving on more than 2,300 flights daily to 130 destinations in 27 countries and two U.S. territories. An intensive two-month course at United's training center at corporate headquarters outside Chicago provided instruction that included survival exercises in a flight simulator. A few restrictions remain—for safety reasons flight attendants must be at least 19 years old and between 5 feet 2 inches and 6 feet in height, and their vision must be correctable to 20/30. They must have a high school diploma or its equivalent, and working experience in the private sector is considered desirable. Because United now flies around the globe, it is also beneficial to speak a second language.

From the days of carrying fuel to the planes, the role of flight attendant has come to encompass just about everything from safety marshal to psychiatrist. As United defines the job, "Flight attendants are responsible for the safety and service of our passengers. Duties include food and beverage service, assisting passengers with disabilities, answering inquiries, and operating mechanical and safety equipment."

Or, as United international flight attendant Debra Waltman explains, "Once a year my job is defined for me at our required Emergency Training in Chicago. It is there that I remember that I am, first and foremost, a trained safety professional with what I feel is the finest airline in the business today." ✈

Mr. Stimpson, if women were casually living in the air, choosing to work there, wouldn't it have a good psychological effect and help rid the public of any fear? —ELLEN CHURCH

ELLEN CHURCH | 69

ELLEN CHURCH'S JOURNEY BEGAN AT THE UNIVERSITY OF MINNESOTA, WHERE SHE EARNED A DEGREE IN NURSING IN 1926. From there she traveled on to San Francisco, becoming an instructor of nurses at the French Hospital. But once she was on her own and earning a living, the adventurer within her surfaced. During World War I, when she was a little girl, she had spent hours watching servicemen learn to fly in a pasture next to her family's farm. She was mesmerized by the wailing engines, the endless takeoffs and landings. She wanted to be a part of it all. And so one day a decade later, Church went down to the little airfield near San Francisco Bay, pulled out her wallet, and asked for flying lessons. Soon she was wheeling and soaring over the peninsula, an aviator in the making. But female pilots were excluded from the fledgling air carriers. Commercial aviation was a man's world.

That changed in 1930. Church was window-shopping downtown when she came upon the Boeing Air Transport office and read promotions about its new Model 80A passenger transports. She walked in. Because it was a holiday, manager Steve Stimpson was alone without much to do. So the two struck up a conversation about aviation and air travel. It was then that Church learned the airline was hiring male stewards to attend to passengers in flight. "Why wouldn't a girl with nurse's training do a better job serving lunch and looking after passengers on a plane?" she asked. He agreed and said he would check with headquarters and get back to her. He was good to his word, and before year-end Church and seven other young nurses had begun new careers.

Two years later an automobile accident cut short Church's career on the Main Line, and she returned to nursing full-time. She donned a different set of wings during World War II as an air evacuation nurse retrieving wounded soldiers from combat areas.

Ellen Church was a woman ahead of her time. Back when most women assumed traditional roles, she helped invent a new profession. The "Boeing bug" (above) adorned both lapels of the first stewardess uniform in 1930.

Captain Ellen Church saw service in Africa, England, Italy, France, and Germany and was one of the few women to be awarded Air Medals. She formed friendships with some of the most famous military leaders of the day.

After the war, she returned to nursing, becoming an administrator of Union Hospital in Terre Haute, Indiana, in 1952. She resigned from that position in January 1965, three months after marrying Leonard Marshall, an attorney and president of the Terre Haute First National Bank.

Her adventure came to an end one morning the following August when she was thrown from a horse. She died on August 27, 1965. But the adventure continues today for the thousands of United flight attendants—and countless others around the world—whose profession she helped to create. ✈

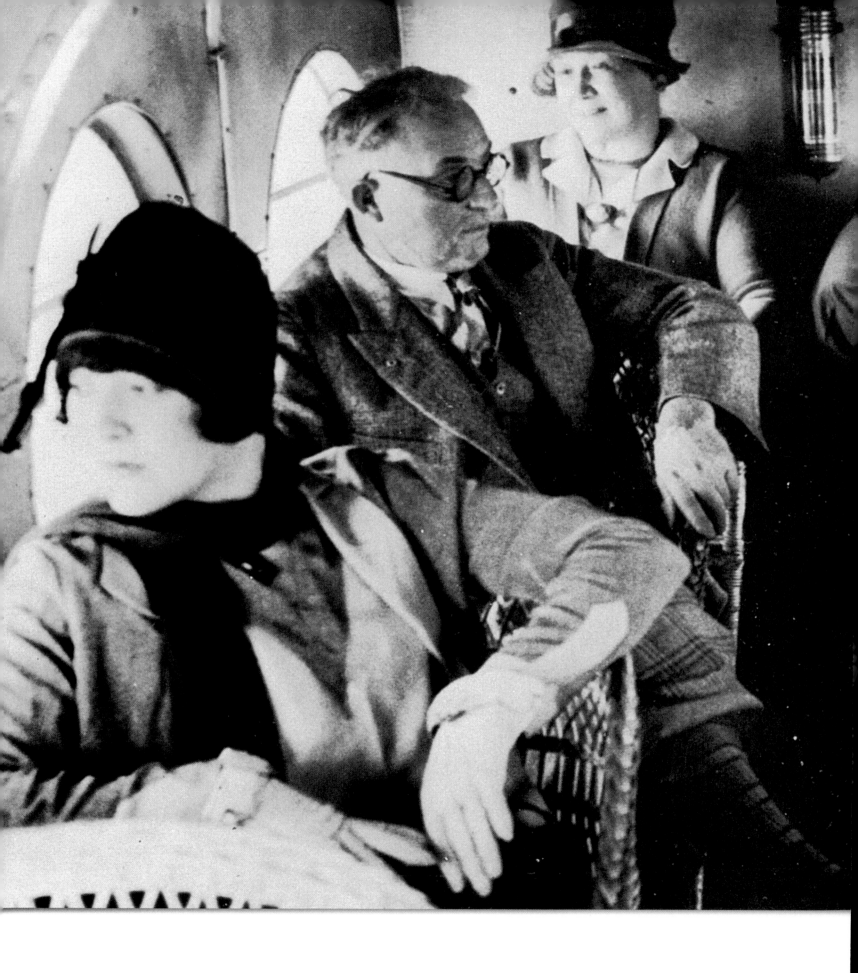

Cigarette smoking only permitted. Throw no matches, lighted cigarettes or refuse on cabin floor or from plane window.

On 1920s planes like this Ford Trimotor, the windows opened but signs urged restraint. A copilot might serve food—and enjoy the view.

For interesting variety no route can equal United's 'Mid-Continent'
with the forested hills, the rolling plains, rivers, lakes and glorious plateaus.
–A 1930s United Ad

A RIDE ON THE MAIN LINE CIRCA 1930 | 73

As the 1920s roared, everything seemed bigger and better and faster. Flappers danced the Charleston and later, the Lindy Hop, named for U.S. aviation hero Charles Lindbergh. Slugger Babe Ruth smashed an incredible 60 home runs in one season. The stock market soared higher and higher. And the "heppest cats" of all bravely took to the skies.

Commercial aviation got a late start in the United States. By the time privately owned companies began carrying sacks of mail in 1926, overseas carriers were making regularly scheduled passenger flights in 17 European countries, as well as on the continents of South America, Australia, and Africa. For the most part, the original U.S. airlines discouraged passengers; indeed most mail planes had no accommodations for them whatsoever. And schedules were so erratic and weather such a nemesis that it was almost impossible to predict when a plane might take off or land—or where it might ultimately end up.

In 1927 mail carriers Boeing Air Transport and National Air Transport joined segments to create the irregularly scheduled first transcontinental passenger service between San Francisco and New York City. The trip was quicker but probably wasn't much more comfortable than riding in the covered wagons that traversed the same route in the previous century. For $404 each, two passengers, donning flying coveralls, parachutes, and goggles, could cram themselves into an enclosed mail pit, sit on the mailbags or hold them in their laps, and then endure a 32-hour, 2,600-mile, 15-stop flight with the engine thundering just a few feet in front of them. And when the benumbed passengers changed airlines and planes in Chicago, they risked losing their seats if additional mail had to be loaded aboard.

In the early 1930s, planes like the Ford Trimotor (left) were inspiring and accommodating— and crossing the continent. United's first crew pin in 1930 (above) featured the Main Line— as did the 1931 route map (following pages).

But within just a few years these early carriers had embraced the inevitability—and potential profitability—of passenger service. In 1929 Boeing and NAT introduced trimotor transports designed specifically to carry 12 to 18 passengers in an enclosed cabin. These faster planes cut the journey to only 28 hours, and increased capacity allowed the airlines to reduce the cross-country fare to $259.50 (about $2,500 in today's dollars). They followed the same route, but what was once known as U.S. Mail Route No. 1 was quickly becoming known across the nation as the Main Line.

While flights were scheduled to leave at a specific time, departure time tended to be flexible. It varied depending on the weather, the availability of the airplane and pilots, and the arrival of the passengers. Many times, an "aero-trailer," a car, picked up passengers in the city and brought them

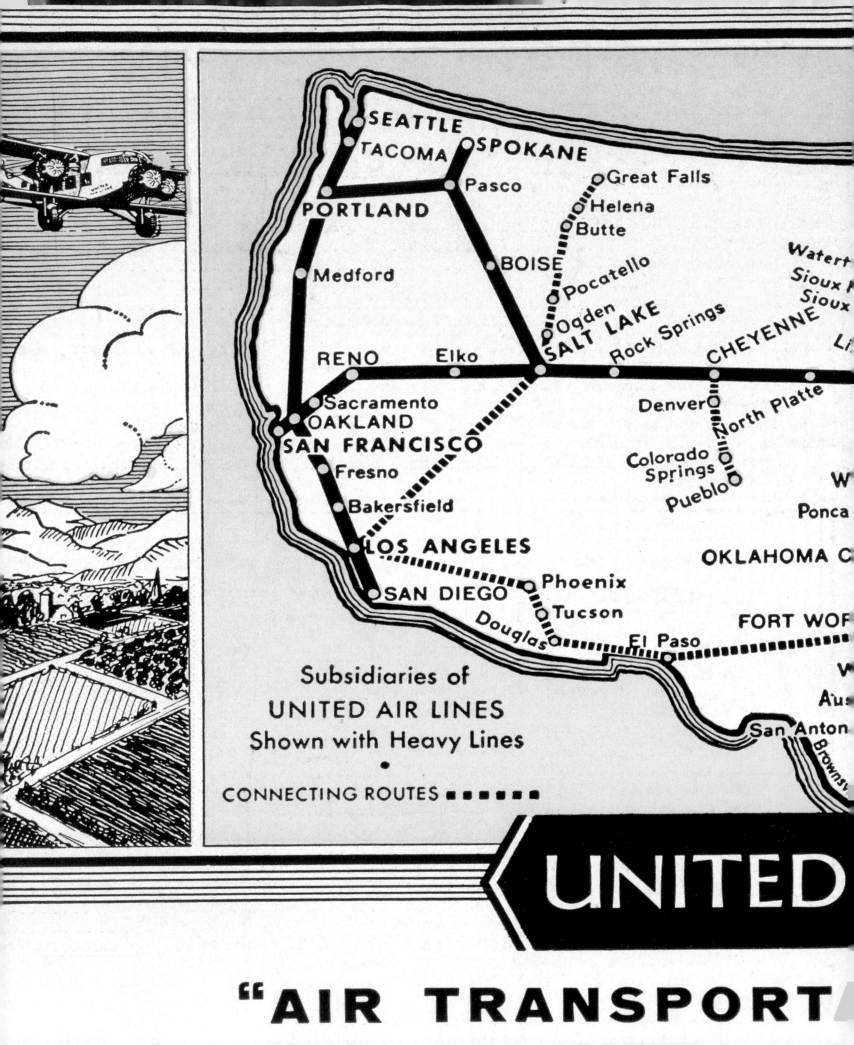

SEATTLE
TACOMA
SPOKANE
Pasco
Great Falls
Helena
Butte
PORTLAND
Medford
BOISE
Pocatello
Watert
Sioux
Sioux
Ogden
SALT LAKE
Rock Springs
CHEYENNE
Li
RENO
Elko
Denver
North Platte
Sacramento
OAKLAND
SAN FRANCISCO
Colorado
Springs
Pueblo
W
Fresno
Ponca
Bakersfield
OKLAHOMA C
LOS ANGELES
Phoenix
SAN DIEGO
Tucson
FORT WOR
Douglas
El Paso
V
A'us
San Anton
Brownsv

Subsidiaries of
UNITED AIR LINES
Shown with Heavy Lines

•

CONNECTING ROUTES ■■■■■■

UNITED

"AIR TRANSPORT

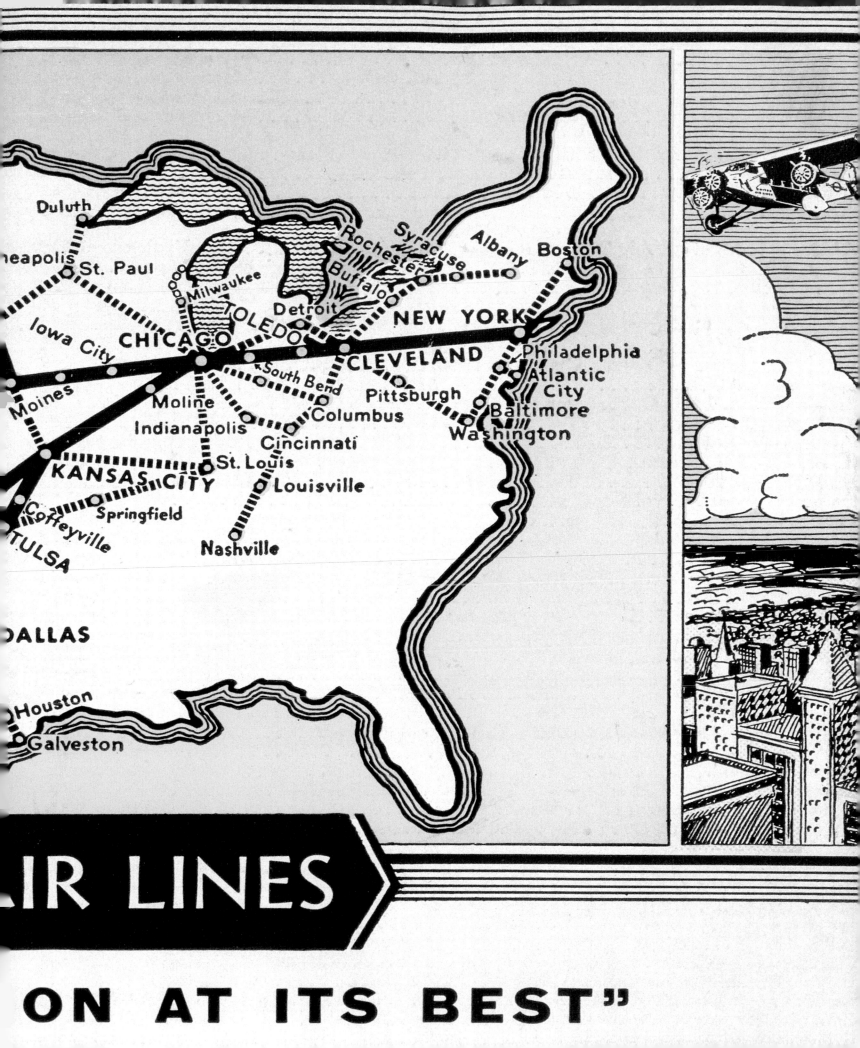

Duluth
neapolis St. Paul
Milwaukee
Iowa City
CHICAGO
TOLEDO
Detroit
Moines
Moline
South Bend
Indianapolis
KANSAS CITY
St. Louis
Coffeyville Springfield
TULSA
Nashville
Louisville
Cincinnati
Columbus
Pittsburgh
Washington

Rochester Syracuse Albany Boston
Buffalo
NEW YORK
CLEVELAND
Philadelphia
Atlantic City
Baltimore

DALLAS

Houston
Galveston

IR LINES

ON AT ITS BEST"

Stewardess service in 1931 (far right) *featured meals and amenities unheard of a few years before. By the mid-1940s, DC-4 flights offered meals on beige plasticware with a design like a captain's insignia.*

to the airport. By 1929, some 80 leading U.S. corporations permitted key employees to put airfares on their expense accounts.

Before departure from San Francisco, passengers' luggage was weighed and tagged, their tickets were collected, and safety regulations were explained. Comfort packages were distributed that included cotton balls for the ears—the engine roar was deafening—and chewing gum for dealing with changes in air pressure. Passengers could carry two bags weighing a total of 25 pounds.

Most flights were still taking off in bright daylight, although the government's nationwide system of lighted airway beacons every 30 miles had been completed. The first stop was Reno, Nevada, two hours away, where planes would meet connecting flights from Los Angeles, San Diego, the Pacific Northwest, and Montana.

The interior of the cabin was designed to resemble a train coach to reassure passengers by putting them in a familiar setting. The mailbags and hard benches passengers had used as seats only two years earlier had been replaced by upholstered chairs. And rather than sitting hunched over in a confined storage space, they now sat in a cabin spacious enough to permit them to walk around.

The uninsulated cabin was chilly in winter and warm in summer, so the windows slid open or rolled down to provide fresh air for the passengers. But open windows also drew engine fumes into the cabin. The biggest problem was the noise of the engines, which made normal conversation impossible. Most planes had toilet facilities, including a small sink with hot and cold running water, but the toilet itself was simply a seat that opened to reveal a hole in the floor.

In the enclosed cockpit the two pilots often referred to their old logbooks, compiled over years and thousands of miles of flying. The books noted all the major landmarks, the compass headings, and the time needed to fly between landmarks on the major routes. In addition to their logbooks, these pilots also had a directed radio beam to mark their course. As long as the pilots stayed on the correct course, they heard a continuously repeated buzz or dash; if they deviated from their course the sound changed to an ominous dot-dash or dash-dot. Every 20 minutes, pilots were required to report their position to the nearest ground station via radiophone and upon doing so received the latest weather information. The trimotors raced over the country at speeds reaching 120 miles per hour, covering more land in eight minutes than the pioneers did with their covered wagons in an entire day. Stops en route included Elko, Nevada; Salt Lake City, Utah; Cheyenne, Wyoming; North Platte and Omaha, Nebraska; Des Moines, Iowa; and finally—20 hours from San Francisco—Chicago, Illinois, the aviation hub of the United States.

Because the cabin wasn't pressurized, the planes had to fly through, rather than over, bad weather, which sometimes forced

ELEV. ABOVE SEA LEVEL 4400 FT.
191 MILES TO SAN FRANCISCO · 2575 MILES TO NEW YORK
RENO

Early pilots flew by visual contact with the ground. In some places, such as Reno, Nevada, and Burbank, California, United owned the airport.

Inflight entertainment on a Ford Trimotor in 1930 (far right) *was limited to the altimeter and outside temperature gauge on the forward bulkhead. The* **"Burp Cup"** (right) *airsickness bag was for those who weren't entertained.*

them to make unscheduled landings. Fortunately, cities small and large across the country had built landing fields hoping to attract some of the more than 60 airlines in the nation. The first concrete runway had been built in Dearborn, Michigan, in 1925 by Henry Ford, but most landing strips were little more than packed dirt. The airports rarely consisted of more than a passenger building, which sometimes included a kitchen. On the nicer fields, planes parked under a roof, permitting passengers to avoid bad weather while moving to and from the terminal. Nevertheless, weather posed continuing challenges. Flights often ended prematurely and passengers had to be transported by car, truck, bus, or even ferry to the nearest railroad station to continue their journey.

There were few amenities onboard. For entertainment, passengers tracked their altitude and speed as they flew, using an altimeter and airspeed indicator mounted on the forward cabin bulkhead. On some flights, male stewards served lunch and cigarettes. This was aviation's "fried-chicken era." The chicken came wrapped in wax paper and was accompanied by a bag of potato chips and a tomato. When frequent fliers began to wonder aloud how many chickens must be consumed before a person would be able to fly without an airplane, the airlines knew they had to expand their inflight menus. So Boeing began serving cold sandwiches and fruit in a papier-mâché box. Coffee and cold water were served from half-pint Thermos bottles.

The meal was supposed to be served on one-legged tables—the leg fit into a hole in the cabin floor and two clips fastened it to the cabin wall—but when rough weather caused plates to slide, passengers put pillows on their laps and put their plates on the pillows. Within a couple of years, Boeing introduced a small shelf that could be used as a lunch table and began serving more elaborate meals, including chicken casserole. Even then, not all passengers felt like eating in the bumpy air at low altitudes.

All transcontinental flights landed at Chicago's Municipal Airport. With eight runways, it had more than any other airport in the nation. NAT passengers arriving in Chicago were given a Certificate of Flight signed by the vice president and general manager of the company to commemorate their adventure. Passengers were also asked to sign the inflight register, much like hotel guests.

After the 20-hour flight from the West Coast to Chicago, New York was less than seven hours away. At least part of this 1,200-mile leg took place at night, when passengers could, for the first time, marvel at the world of lights far below.

Main Line flights landed at Newark, New York City's first major airport. There, weary passengers transferred to more conventional modes of transportation. Air travel was in its infancy, and as these early passengers jostled along by car and train to their final destinations, it's easy to imagine the amazement they surely felt at so suddenly being on the opposite side of the United States.

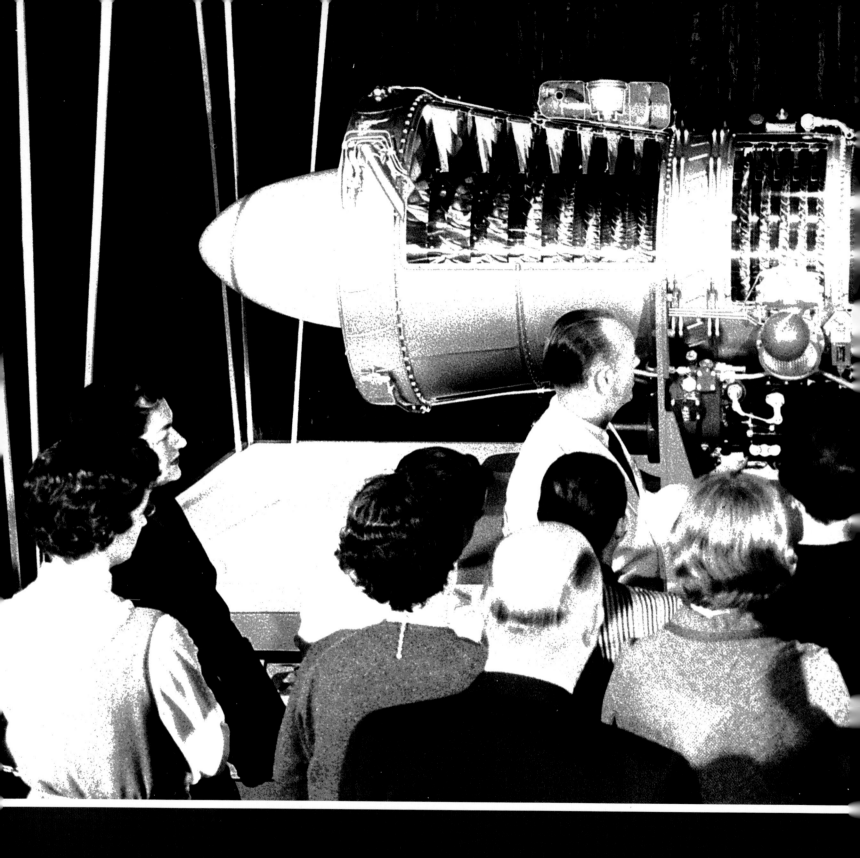

TECHNOLOGICAL ACHIEVEMENTS

So long as the airlines preserve their magic quality—including, above all, their safety and reliability—they will be guaranteed a significant role in the workings of the world. Science will never digitize an embrace. Electronics will never convey the wavering eye of a negotiation adversary. Fiber-optic cable can do many things but cannot transport hot sand, fast snow, or great ruins. –THOMAS PETZINGER JR., *HARD LANDING*

CONQUERING THE ELEMENTS | 85

PAT PATTERSON'S "RULE OF FIVE" WASN'T JUST A CORPORATE SLOGAN. SAFETY, PASSENGER COMFORT, DEPENDABILITY, honesty, and sincerity were watchwords carefully followed on the way to turning United into one of the world's great airlines. Safety led that list, and Patterson's United invested heavily in research and development that enhanced the entire industry—a commitment that has made United a leader in technology throughout its 75-year history.

One of the earliest efforts to increase safety was the establishment of the industry's only Communications Laboratory. It was founded in 1929 by Thorp Hiscock and it developed, among many devices, the first practical two-way radio, permitting pilots to speak with people on the ground.

An outgrowth of that effort and often forgotten in aviation history is United's "flying laboratory." The twin-engine Boeing 247-D, registration number NX13365, was a passenger plane taken out of regular service in early 1937. Seats were removed, workbenches and other pieces of equipment were installed, and it was designated for "flight research." As the first true flying laboratory, the 365 contributed more to the early technological development of commercial aviation than any other airplane.

Although pilots could talk to people on the ground, radio static often interfered. United line pilot Albert Ball and test pilot Benny Howard rigged the 365 with a length of wire that trailed from the aircraft's tail. A small paper cup at the end of the wire kept it taut. The pilots discovered that the trailing wire would collect static from the aircraft's metal surfaces and discharge it into the atmosphere, thus reducing radio interference. The first reliable static eliminator was the result.

A mid-1920s airmail pilot studies weather conditions in a dispatch office (left). *United's "flying laboratory," the industry's first, helped develop the radio altimeter that replaced the altitude barometer* (above).

For almost a decade the 365 was used by United scientists and engineers—as well as by those from aircraft, instrument, and radio manufacturers, the military, the National Advisory Committee for Aeronautics, and the Civil Aeronautics Administration—to test an extraordinary variety of equipment intended to make flying safer and more comfortable. When lab engineers wanted to test the first gyro-controlled automatic pilot, they installed it in the 365. Other 365 assignments included the development of wing and propeller deicers, variable-pitch propellers, radio direction finders, a switchboard system for changing frequencies, pressure injection carburetors, compasses, and various kinds of communications antennas.

The radio altimeter was tested on the 365. It used the bounce-back time of short radio waves to

The researchers who staffed United's "flying lab" were the perfect expression of the airline's early mission to make aviation safe—even routine. The instrument-packed lab, a Boeing 247-D (right), helped perfect a wealth of key technologies.

determine actual clearance above the ground rather than using air pressure to compute altitude above sea level—a critical advance for flying over mountains. The "flight analyzer," precursor to the much more compact and complex device called the "black box" or flight data recorder, was developed and tested aboard the 365. The original flight analyzer recorded aircraft heading, speed, and altitude, and United was the first airline to install the device on its entire fleet.

Early in 1942, the 365 was drafted into military service by the Army's Aircraft Radio Laboratory. United's engineers had been working to develop a reliable automated instrument landing system, and that work continued throughout the war. Army officials estimated that the aircraft made several thousand landings to test military equipment that eventually would be installed at airfields around the world.

During the war the laboratory was also used in the development of radar systems and early "smart bombs"—weapons that could be dropped from one plane and guided to their target by another one flying safely out of antiaircraft gun range. During this period, rudimentary television equipment was installed aboard the aircraft to broadcast a view of the landing in thick fog. The scene was televised to support crews on the ground as it was unfolding.

By the conclusion of the war, the 365 had logged tens of thousands of miles and played an important role in the development of systems that were making flight safe and comfortable. The research performed on that airplane had saved more lives than anyone then living would ever appreciate.

United's continuing research developed the industry's first Instrument Landing System (ILS) and weather radar, which allowed pilots to chart the safest course. Under Patterson's direction, United became the first airline to use electronic flight simulators, which greatly improved flight training, and the first to employ electronic computers to map out the safest and most fuel-efficient flight path. After Patterson's retirement, United became the first airline to install production-quality collision avoidance systems, and its DC-8s were the first to qualify under the FAA's strict all-weather landing program.

Another United aircraft, a Boeing 747SP, has taken to the skies on a mission that would surely make one proud grandpa out of old 365. United's global support business, United Services, is assisting NASA and DLR, the German Aerospace Center, with plans to explore the heavens. Using the aircraft as a platform, SOFIA, the Stratospheric Observatory for Infrared Astronomy, will operate a new generation of infrared telescope from an altitude high above the water vapor that clouds earthbound observations.

The aircraft, which originally operated as Pan Am's Clipper *Lindbergh*, had been in long-term storage when purchased for the project. It is fitted with a telescope 8 feet in diameter and special doors that open in flight to permit observations.

After selecting the United liner, project organizers then chose the airline to be a SOFIA team member. United maintains the aircraft at NASA's Ames Research Center near Mountain View, California, and at the airline's huge overhaul facilities in nearby San Francisco and Oakland. Specially trained United pilots fly the jumbo jet observatory on 120–140 research flights annually.

SOFIA's explorations could continue for another 20 years after its start in 2002. And while its discoveries won't make flying faster or more comfortable, they will expand our knowledge of the universe and perhaps point the way to the stars—a possibility the crews and technicians aboard old 365 might never have imagined but most certainly would have cheered. ///

YOUR

JEPPESEN COMPUTER

MODEL R-2

I didn't start out to chart the skies; it's just no one had done it before.

— E. B. JEPPESEN

ELREY JEPPESEN AND THORP HISCOCK | 89

ELREY JEPPESEN / IN AVIATION'S EARLY YEARS, PILOTS HAD LITTLE INFORMATION AND ALMOST NO INSTRUMENTATION to get them through fog and foul weather and safely to their destinations. They relied on experience, instinct, and luck. Those who were lacking in any of the three often paid for the deficiency with their lives. One young airman named Elrey Borge Jeppesen was determined to put the odds of becoming an old airman in his favor.

Young "Jepp" Jeppesen had once used money he saved from delivering newspapers and groceries to pay for a ride in a barnstormer's Curtiss Jenny biplane. The year was 1921, and he was 14. When he alighted eight minutes later, with the sound of the wind thrumming through the wire struts still in his ears, he was hooked. He began taking flying lessons.

By Jeppesen's senior year in high school, aviation's allure was irresistible. He quit school, used the money he'd accumulated to buy an old Jenny and, with the support of his parents—whom he'd previously regarded as starchy, old-country Danes—he set off as a barnstormer. For a time he flew with a flying circus, doing stunt flying and wing walking, and then he worked his way south, becoming an aerial survey pilot over the Mississippi Delta and Mexico. He later flew for Varney, then Boeing Air Transport, and ultimately with United.

At first Jeppesen was a copilot on the trimotor Boeing 80s; then he graduated to the single-engine, one-pilot Boeing 40s. He'd navigate by Rand McNally road maps and, when weather worsened, he'd descend below the clouds and find his way by "hugging the U-P"—following the tracks of the Union Pacific Railroad.

Jeppesen's later hand-held computers gave pilots a convenient way to make a variety of flight calculations. And the manual gave readers a laugh (left). *The radio headset* (above) *was used by United DC-3 pilots in the 1940s.*

For those who lived the experience, the romance of the open-cockpit era was chilled by the unheated aircraft and the steady toll of fallen comrades—four of the 18 pilots assigned with Jeppesen to the Oakland-Cheyenne route were killed in one winter's flying.

Jeppesen decided to improve the odds. He began taking photographs and making sketches of the landmarks along his route and recorded the information in a 10-cent loose-leaf notebook. He climbed smokestacks and took measurements. At one point he strapped on three altimeters and climbed Blythe Mountain just east of Salt Lake City to ascertain its true altitude. He drove from Chicago to Oakland, taking measure of the emergency fields, the nearby obstructions, and the best approaches. He solicited data from county engineers, surveyors, farmers—anyone who might

DEPICTING TWO-WAY VOICE
RADIOPHONE COMMUNICATION
BETWEEN PLANES AND GROUND

Inventions by United's **Thorp Hiscock** (right) *and* **charts created by Elrey Jeppesen** (left) *contributed greatly to safety. A 1930s post card* (preceding pages) *explained the wonder of air to ground communications—technology pioneered by United.*

92

be able to add detail to the notes thickening his little book.

With this information Jeppesen began to devise the safest ways to locate and land in various airfields, procedures that would ultimately be adopted and published by the federal government. Soon word spread that Jeppesen had written down the information that could get you home, and pilots began asking for copies of his notes. When the number of requests became steady, he sold reprints of his notebook for $10 a copy. And the requests kept coming.

Jeppesen's aeronautical charting business grew as more and more pilots learned about his airway manual and "let-down charts." Finally, in 1954, Jeppesen—by then a United DC-6 pilot—resigned from the airline to devote himself full-time to his basement business. When he sold the company seven years later, it was billing $5 million annually and had become one of the world's foremost purveyors of printed and electronic aeronautical information. In 2000, Boeing purchased its former pilot's company for $1.5 billion.

Captain E.B. Jeppesen died in 1996, just months after the death of his wife, Nadine, one of the early Boeing Air Transport stewardesses. Today, a statue of the aviator looks down on the comings and goings of travelers in the main passenger terminal—the Elrey B. Jeppesen Terminal—at Denver International Airport. In the exhibit cases below the bronze pilot, visitors can see Jeppesen's rough charts and notes scrawled in tattered notebooks.

THORP HISCOCK / Legend has it that one evening a former World War I flight instructor named Thorp Hiscock was either dining with his brother-in-law, Bill Boeing, or working in his radio shop in Yakima, Washington, when he heard the story of an airmail pilot en route from Omaha to North Platte. The pilot either was killed in a crash or made a safe but forced landing after the weather ahead of him changed suddenly and there was no way he could be notified. The visibility became so bad, the story goes, that he couldn't even see the red flares sent up or the bonfires lit on the ground, the methods then used to warn pilots of bad weather ahead.

Exactly what inspired Hiscock may be in question, but there's no argument that he decided to solve this supposedly unsolvable problem by inventing a two-way radio that would permit pilots to communicate with a crew on the ground.

The Wright brothers proved we could fly, but men like Thorp Hiscock made flying safe. After leaving the Army Air Corps, the former banker from upstate New York became a hops rancher and then opened a radio shop in Yakima. Until he tackled the air-to-ground communication problem, pilots navigated by following mapped landmarks like trees, rivers, church steeples, and buildings—sometimes even cutting their engines and shouting questions to people on the ground. Many engineers believed two-way radio communication between pilots and people on the ground was impractical.

When Hiscock joined Boeing in 1928, he set up a transmitter in a hangar, installed a receiver in an automobile, and drove farther and farther from that base each day until he had identified the most efficient radio frequencies. Then he directed the construction of an airplane, working with radio engineers to shield each component to cut down on interference. In 1929, 38-pound short-wave receivers were installed in every Boeing plane. Two-way radio between the air and the ground had become a reality.

That was only the beginning of Hiscock's meteoric career as head of United's vaunted Communications Laboratory. When Hiscock found a problem that intrigued him, he attacked it forcefully, sometimes living for days in the lab, often existing only on popcorn. At that time, pilots were completely at the mercy of the elements; pressurized cabins, heated cockpits, wing deicers, and automated pilot and landing systems were simply dreams. Hiscock set out to make many of them come true.

Ice accumulating on wings was one of the pilots' greatest fears. Hiscock invented a rudimentary deicer by affixing a series of long rubber tubes to the leading edge of the wing. He realized that inflating and deflating the device caused it to contract and expand, preventing ice from collecting and shedding ice that did accumulate. Hiscock worked with B.F. Goodrich Tire and Rubber Company to perfect the design.

While Hiscock's inventions could have been used to give United a competitive edge, they were made available to the entire aviation industry, greatly improving safety for everyone.

In the quest to develop a reliable autopilot, three different companies had patented systems, but none of them was completely successful. Hiscock managed to gain the cooperation of all three companies and used the best elements of each system to create the first successful "robot pilot."

The list of his accomplishments is remarkable and long. Thorp Hiscock developed the first practical propeller pitch controls and an automated fuel-injection system that fed the proper fuel mix to engines at any altitude. In 1934, while working on ways to pressurize and heat passenger cabins, as well as developing equipment for instrument landings and even a one-button takeoff and landing system, 41-year-old Thorp Hiscock died of a heart attack. ⚑

A 1930s promotional photo made the point that United's Boeing 247s were flying the same Main Line route followed west by the pioneers.

FLY TO RENO FOR YOUR WEDDING

In 1933, Boeing's 247 set the aviation world on fire. It was the world's first modern airplane—the plane that revolutionized commercial aviation. Every passenger plane made today has a lot of the 247 in its DNA.
—DR. ROBERT VAN DER LINDEN, CURATOR OF AIR TRANSPORTATION, SMITHSONIAN'S NATIONAL AIR AND SPACE MUSEUM

THE BOEING 247 | 97

IT WAS BILL BOEING'S CROWNING ACHIEVEMENT, THE WONDER OF THE AGE, AND MORE. NOT ONLY DID THE MODEL 247 make everything else in the sky obsolete, but it also certified the manifest triumph of Boeing's all-encompassing conglomerate—it was nothing less than the future of aviation.

At the outset of the 1930s, the mainstay passenger transports of the fledgling airlines were an assortment of homely craft—Boeing's trimotored Model 80 among them—characterized by boxy fuselages, wicker seats, fixed landing gear, metal or wood frames, and skins of stretched cloth or aluminum sheets corrugated for extra strength. These slow and noisy airplanes hardly offered an ideal passenger experience.

Meanwhile, Boeing was at work on a streamlined, all-metal bomber that proved to be faster than the Army's best fighters. Although the military chose another aircraft, Boeing had confidence in its new design and began adapting it for carrying passengers. The resulting aircraft, the Boeing 247, was unlike anything that had ever gone into commercial service. It featured a low, cantilevered wing, metal skin that added to the strength of the aircraft, and landing gear that retracted during flight to reduce drag. Inside, the cabin featured five seats with fixed arm rests spaced a generous 40 inches apart on either side of a single aisle. Aft there was a galley and restroom.

Prominent on the 247's wings was a pair of cowled Pratt & Whitney Wasp engines, each turning a gleaming Hamilton Standard propeller. The engines' combined output of 1,100 horsepower, together with the aircraft's remarkably clean design, helped it reach a

Comfortable and quiet, United's Boeing 247s marked the coming of age of commercial aviation (left). This 1930s post card (above) urged people to fly to Reno for the wedding. It generated attention but not many customers.

top cruising speed of nearly 170 mph, 30–50 mph faster than the trimotors that were its principal competition. It could fly coast to coast in less than a day.

The aircraft was an instant sensation; "Born a Queen" was one journalist's description of the new Boeing. Chicago's "Century of Progress" exhibition in the summer of 1933 showcased a 247 as the country's latest technological triumph.

United saw the 247 as an aircraft that would combine passenger comfort with the speed necessary to service the heavily subsidized airmail contracts, which in those early days of commercial aviation were the main source of airline profits. In fact, says Dr. Robert van der Linden, curator of air transportation at the Smithsonian's National Air and Space Museum, "The 247 was first

UNITED
AIR LINES

New Type All-Metal Wasp-Powered
"Three-Mile-A-Minute" Boeing Transport
displayed in the Dome of the TRAVEL AND
TRANSPORT BUILDING, Chicago, 1933

Climaxing
A CENTURY OF PROGRESS
IN TRANSPORTATION

Two supercharged Wasp engines gave United's Boeing 247 unprecedented speed. It wowed the crowds at Chicago's "Century of Progress."

The streamlined 247 inspired this promotional lamp for United employees in 1933. Even at $10.95, the now rare Depression-era luxury item soon sold out (above). **Film starlets welcomed the plane's 1933 appearance in Los Angeles** (far right).

designed as a high-speed, eight-passenger mail plane, then morphed into a 10-passenger airliner."

In 1932, United agreed to purchase 60 of the new planes for its four carriers for a staggering $4 million, thus assuring itself operational exclusivity while guaranteeing Boeing profitability and full production for months. United took delivery of its first 247 in March 1933 and proceeded to advertise its unprecedented speed to the hilt, touting that its new plane would "fly you across the continent in a single night." And since the 247 could operate at altitudes of up to 8,000 feet, higher than any of its predecessors, United informed passengers that they could now "fly over winter."

Paradoxically, the corporate connection between United and Boeing proved to be the airplane's undoing. When other carriers tried to order the 247, they were told they'd have to wait until all the United planes had been delivered.

Unwilling to suffer years of competitive disadvantage, other airlines turned to the Douglas Aircraft Company in hopes that the California firm could produce a machine to counter the 247. Douglas accepted the challenge and, just three months after United took delivery of its first 247, the DC-1 was airborne. That aircraft would quickly evolve into the DC-2 and then the DC-3. Both planes were so superior to the 247 in every way that, despite an upgrade in engines and other refinements, the sleek Boeing was done for. United's eagle had been transformed into a turkey.

By 1935, Bill Boeing's unprecedented aviation conglomerate had been disassembled by federal edict. Unfettered and independent, United Air Lines did the unthinkable by purchasing 10 DC-3s, the first of scores it would eventually place in service. As the years passed, it used its 247s on lesser routes or farmed them out to smaller carriers that delivered passengers to its Main Line. In the end, Douglas produced 11,000 DC-3s and their military equivalents, while United was the only major operator of the 247s, and fewer than 80 were ever built.

Its reign was brief, but United's 247 was an epochal aircraft. It was the first modern airliner, a breakthrough design to which every succeeding prop plane and jetliner could trace a part of its heritage. And while United was disappointed by its experience with the 247, the airline nevertheless went on to introduce other significant and far more successful aircraft into domestic service, including the Douglas DC-8, the Boeing 720, 737, 767, and, most significant, the mammoth 777 intercontinental twinjet. ✈

NOTICE

Your Plane is Scheduled to Depart

From the .... Airport

City .... State

Time .... Date

PLEASE WAIT FOR ATTENDANT TO ASSIS

LAST

Have you advi
Have you mad
Have you purc
Has your bagg
If your journe
modations been a
on connecting lir

If your trip is
rest room before

Every possible
fort en route. If y
provide a good re

The Station At
plane when reac
warmed up in ord
readiness. After
enjoy one of the

INUTE SUGGESTIONS

ve you forgotten anything?

our friends where to meet you?

r hotel reservations?

d that home-coming gift?

een properly checked?

be continued by train or boat have your accom-
ged for? If by air, we will gladly make reservation
you.

of any length at all, we suggest that you visit the
ng.

enience is provided in each plane for your com-
e troubled with travel sickness our attendants will
y prior to departure.

nt will arrange a platform and help you into the
depart. Please stand by while motor is being
at plane may be dispatched when everything is in
ng into the plane, relax, lean back and prepare to
pleasant trips of your life.

OU TO ALIGHT ON ARRIVAL AT STATION

Today, computer engineers consider Instamatic the Model T of cybernetics. And like the Model T, Instamatic proved itself for reliability, piling up a 99.8 percent up-time record during its 11 years of 24-hour daily operation. It was the fastest and most accurate system of its kind ever developed.
—DONALD LARSON, PRESIDENT OF UNITED'S COMPUTER SERVICES DIVISION

A TICKET TO RIDE

IN THE EARLY DAYS OF AVIATION, THERE WERE NO FLIGHT RESERVATIONS. A PILOT SET DOWN IN A FARMER'S FIELD OR at the fairgrounds, and people lined up and paid cash to experience the thrill of flight. Until the late 1920s the airlines discouraged passenger service because their revenue was derived from carrying the mail for the government. But more-powerful airplanes allowed airlines to carry paying passengers in addition to the mail.

In 1926, for example, passengers could "accompany mail bags" from Los Angeles to Seattle for $132; 10 years later a passenger could fly coast to coast for $150. When the airlines began following regular schedules to distant destinations, a system had to be established to reserve seats on specific flights. For the first time, passengers needed flight reservations.

At first, ticketing and reservations were very informal. In some instances, an agent sat at a desk right next to the plane, selling and taking tickets as passengers boarded. The actual ticket was adapted from the railroads, listing all the cities where the airline flew, and the cities of origin and destination were simply hand-punched. In 1930 the ticket did not guarantee the passenger would arrive at his destination, warning, "If in the judgment of the Company agents, pilots or employees it is not deemed safe to proceed ... the Company may cancel the balance of the trip and refund the part of fare equal to the unused portion of this ticket." The airline also had the right to leave the passenger "in any such place as the pilot or other agent of the company may ... see fit."

The envelope in which the ticket was delivered also reminded passengers, "If your trip is to be of any length at all, we suggest you visit the restroom before leaving," and promised, "If you are troubled with travel sickness our attendants will provide a good remedy prior to departure."

The San Francisco traffic (ticket) office in the 1930s (left). Steve Stimpson the co-founder of stewardess service stands in the background on the right. The sticker (above) and ticket wallet cover (preceding pages) come from the same romantic era.

As the planes carried few passengers, there was only one class of service and everyone paid the same fare, although on some airlines roundtrip tickets purchased in advance garnered a 10 percent discount. And while there were no credit cards, frequent flyers could purchase airline scrip, which looked a bit like Monopoly money and could be used to purchase tickets on most domestic airlines. The air scrip books contained tickets worth $500 but could be bought for considerably less.

Commercial aviation grew dramatically in the 1930s; by mid-decade, the nation's airlines had carried millions of passengers, and a better system of reserving seats had to be created. In the 1950s United's reservation system was using the most advanced technology available: people and

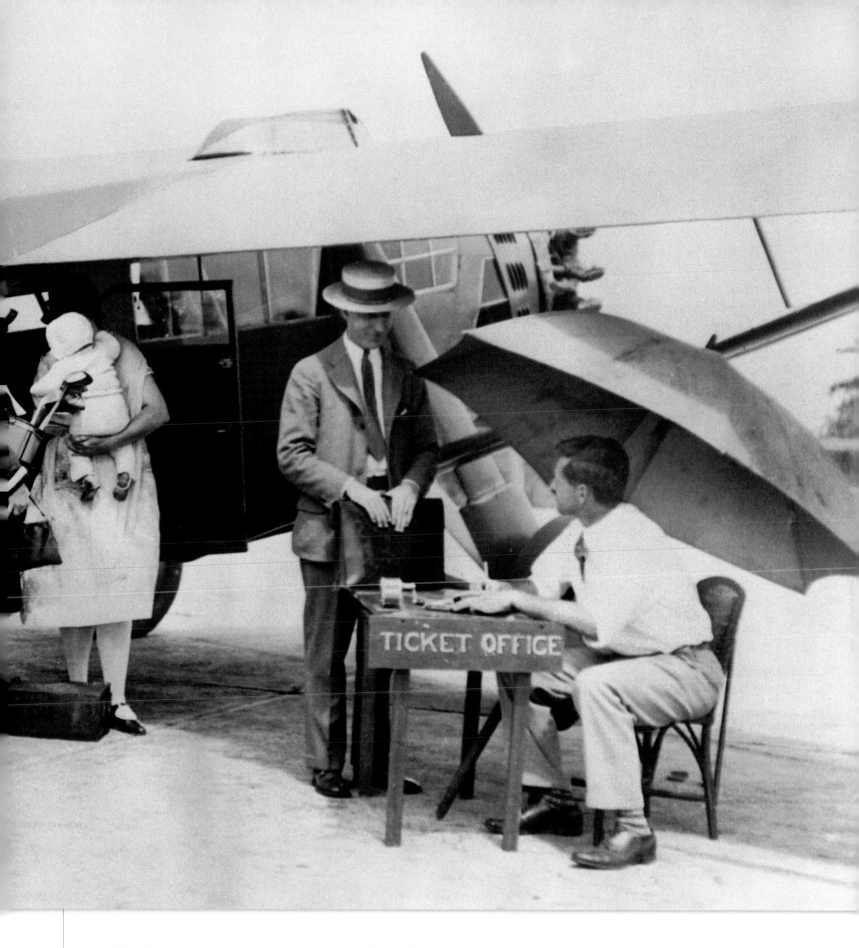

These 1920s National Air Transport passengers visited a "ticket office" reminiscent of today's Chariot ᔆᴹ mobile check-in units.

Early passenger tickets plainly stated the terms of passage (right). *As the airlines aspired to rail-style comfort—and the same level of passenger confidence—Boeing Air Transport used punches to cancel tickets. Employees even called out, "All aboard."*

telephones. Reservations were taken over the phone and handwritten records were kept on file. Seat sales were reported verbally to a central inventory center in Denver. The availability of seats on certain flights for the next 30 days was manually posted on a large board in the office. Availability for all other flights and dates was recorded in the local office availability book. Tickets were mailed to travelers or could be picked up at ticket offices or travel agencies.

The tickets had evolved, too. The long, narrow, cardboard ticket with the passenger's origin and destination preprinted on each coupon was introduced in 1946. This saved considerable time, as it was no longer necessary for the agent to write that information on each of several coupons. And travelers could buy tickets on a "Fly now—pay later" installment plan.

Early in 1955 United introduced Unisel, a machine that looked a bit like an adding machine and for the first time allowed agents in large reservations offices to mechanically check the availability of flights over the next 30 days. Within another year, Unisel allowed agents to key in the number of seats sold on a specific flight, although the details of each reservation still had to be recorded and processed on punch cards. It was a slow, unwieldy system.

In 1961 United introduced the $16 million Instamatic system, the largest electronic data-processing system ever built for private industry. It allowed reservations agents in any U.S. office to book or cancel space on any United flight within the next year.

Fares were changing, too. In 1963, in an attempt to eliminate confusing multi-class, multi-fare flights, Chairman/CEO Pat Patterson introduced "One Class Service" priced between first class and coach. Competitors met this plan by lowering their own first-class fares to just above one-class fares. United countered by introducing "Red, White and Blue" (first class, standard, and coach) sections on selected flights. Add the impact of growing passenger traffic, and reservations systems could barely keep pace.

Then in March 1971, United's computerized system Apollo allowed agents to check availability, make reservations, and store passenger name records. Apollo became the standard of the entire industry. The true value of the new system became apparent several years later when the U.S. government regulation of fares ended. That led to the introduction of the present sliding time- and seat-availability pricing approach. With earlier systems, it would have been impossible to keep track of all the options available to passengers.

The ticket delivery process, which had remained "by mail or pick-up" for decades, changed drastically in the 1990s. In 1994 United became the first carrier to offer the electronic ticket to replace the traditional paper ticket. Computer technology allowed customers to make reservations online—without speaking to an agent—or by phone and then pick up their boarding passes when they arrived at the airport. By the beginning of the 21st century, 60 percent of United's passengers were using E-Tickets[SM].

In April 1995, the United Connection was introduced; it allowed travelers using personal computers to make reservations on more than 500 airlines, at 30,000 hotels, and with 50 car rental companies. And the United Connection remembered customer preferences, including seat and meal selection, hotel features, and a variety of other special needs.

In 2000 the Permanent Research Collection on Information Technology at the Smithsonian Institution honored United for its innovative electronic ticketing software, which was by then being used by 14 different airlines.

Full Thru Fare, $ _165__

From **San Francisco (S. F. Airport)**

To **New York (Newark Airport)**

ONE WAY ~~ROUND TRIP~~

CROSS OUT ONE OF ABOVE

Via **BOEING AIR TRANSPORT**

Via **NATIONAL AIR TRANSPORT**

Date **OCT 12 1933**

_7 20_ A.M.
P.M. Seat No. _____

AIR PASSAGE CONTRACT

In consideration of the issuance of this ticket the purchaser agrees to the following conditions:

NON-TRANSFERABLE: This ticket is non-transferable.

DATE VALID: This ticket is valid only for passage beginning on the date shown on the face of the ticket and for the plane and seat specified therein.

REFUNDS: To entitle the holder to a refund on this ticket if not used it must be surrendered to the Company at least two hours in advance of the departure of the plane for which this ticket is issued. Refunds will be made only from the head office of the Company. Post Office Box OO, Chicago, Ill.

UNCOMPLETED FLIGHTS: After the commencement of the flight the passenger may be landed and discharged in such manner and in such place as the pilot of the plane or other agent of the Company may in their sole discretion see fit, and in that event the sole responsibility of the Company shall be to refund to the passenger such proportion of the price of this ticket as the distance between the place of landing and the place of destination bears to the whole length of the flight for which this ticket was issued.

BAGGAGE: 30 pounds of baggage will be carried free on each full fare ticket. All baggage in excess of 30 pounds shall be charged an excess rate, as published in tariffs of the Company. The liability of the Company for loss or damage to baggage or other personal property is limited to the amount of $100, unless a higher valuation be declared in advance and an additional charge paid therefor.

AGENCY: The Company issuing this ticket is not responsible beyond its own lines and in selling this ticket and/or checking baggage beyond its own lines the issuing Company acts solely as agent for the transport Company or Companies operating such other lines.

ISSUED BY
BOEING AIR TRANSPORT, INC.
UNITED AIR LINES SYSTEM

Form 502

BOEING AIR TRANSPORT, Inc.

U.S. AIR MAIL

Transcontinental PASSENGER SERVICE

NON-TRANSFERABLE TICKET

Good subject to following contract between purchaser and Boeing Air Transport, Inc., via scheduled route between points punched within thirty days of purchase.

NON-TRANSFERABLE TICKET—If presented by any person other than original purchaser, this ticket will be void and may be confiscated by action of the agent of the Boeing Air Transport, Inc.

BAGGAGE—Each passenger is permitted to carry free 25 pounds of baggage. All baggage in excess of 25 pounds will be charged excess rate. The Company assumes no liability for loss or damage to baggage.

STOP-OVERS—Stop-overs will be permitted at the option of the Transport Company, but resumption of trip is subject to previous reservations of other passengers.

CANCELLATION AND DELAYS—The passenger agrees with the Company that if, in the judgment of the Company agents, pilots or employees, it is not deemed safe to proceed farther with the passenger, that the Company may cancel the balance of the trip and refund the part of fare equal to the unused portion of this ticket.

The Company assumes no responsibility for delay due to any cause whatsoever.

W. G. Herron
V. Pres in chg of Traffic.

CASH FARE PAID			From	To
DOLLARS		**CENTS**	◀ N FRANCISCO, CAL.	
			SACRAMENTO, CAL.	
$ 40	$1	5 55	RENO, NEVADA	
50	2	10 60	ELKO, NEVADA	
60	3	15 65	SALT LAKE CITY, UTAH*	
70	4	20 70	ROCK SPRINGS, WYOM.	
80	5	25 75	CHEYENNE, WYOM.*	
90	6	30 80	NORTH PLATTE, NEB.	
100	7	35 85	OMAHA, NEB.*	
	8	40 90	DES MOINES, IOWA	
300	9	45 95	IOWA CITY, IOWA	
400	10	50	CHICAGO, ILLINOIS	
500	20 30			

PILOT PUNCH THROUGH
OPERATING DIVISIONS
☞ 2 3 4

*Division Point.

I accept the above conditions.

_____
Passenger's Signature.

Street Address _110 Meyer St._

City _San Francisco_

Witness: _____

244

Agent.

Someday people all over this nation and all over the world will fly everywhere. Someday we'll be carrying great loads of freight. Someday (airplanes will) displace the trains. —CHARLES LINDBERGH

THE SILENT PASSENGER

SOON AFTER THE WRIGHT BROTHERS PROVED FLIGHT WAS POSSIBLE, THE MILITARY BEGAN TRANSFORMING FLYING machines into airborne weapons, and merchants dreamed of ways to turn them into flying freight cars. Throughout history, commerce had always been limited by the ability to get products to market. Maine lobsters couldn't survive the long railroad trip to the California coast. California avocados rotted long before reaching New York. But that all began to change on November 7, 1910.

On that day the Morehouse Martens Company of New York City shipped five bolts of silk, weighing 60 pounds and valued at $1,000, to its department store in Columbus, Ohio. What made this order so unusual was that the company decided to ship by rail *and* air. This was the first recorded cargo flight. Coming only seven years after the Wright brothers' first flight, the attempt to deliver goods by air captured the public's imagination.

A company executive carried the silk across his knees on an express train from New York to Dayton, Ohio. He then took his seat on a spartan Wright biplane along with pilot Phil O. Parmalee, who had been taught to fly by Orville Wright, and held on tightly to his package for the 65-mile, 66-minute flight to Columbus. The silk was eventually cut and sewn into men's ties, each of which bore a label proclaiming that it had been fashioned from the first recorded air express shipment.

Newspapers enthusiastically recorded each shipment of goods delivered by air. On January 12, 1914, for example, pilot Tony Janus carried a rush shipment of hams and bacon from Tampa to St. Petersburg Florida, on a "flying boat," a seaplane. The package actually arrived before a telegram informing the recipient to expect it.

The airmail idea quickly caught on, and it didn't take long for the luxury of rapid delivery to become a necessity. The airlines took on cargo, even added dedicated freighters. The emblem above symbolized an urgent new era.

But shipping goods by air remained merely a public relations gimmick until 1927—most of the early planes simply could not carry both the mail and heavy cargo. And at a cost of $3 per pound, air transport was a luxury few shippers could afford. On September 1, 1927, Boeing and National Air Transport joined with American Railway Express Company to form the first coast-to-coast air express service. The first shipments East were sent to President Calvin Coolidge at the White House and included a strip of bacon, a box of fruit, and life masks of Hollywood movie stars. The first plane from Chicago to the West Coast carried a 10-gallon hat for humorist Will Rogers. "Received first hat ever sent by air," Rogers replied. "There has been a lot of them blown off and left by air but not sent purposely."

United's first mechanized air freight depot, a conveyor-belted wonder, opened in Chicago in 1958. Today United carries 3 billion tons of cargo. The airline's expanding fleet of aircraft with generous cargo holds has hastened the end of the dedicated cargoliner.

112

A year later, airfreight had become almost commonplace; in 1928, there were 17,000 shipments sent by airplane. After declining slightly during the Depression, the cargo business began growing again and has not stopped. As planes grew larger and the number of flights increased, rates dropped. Business increased so rapidly that, in 1940, United became the first airline to offer all-cargo flights between the East Coast and the Midwest. In 1946 United set up an Air Cargo Department.

World War II tested the ability of airlines to move massive quantities of men and equipment rapidly and efficiently. The lessons learned were put into practice in the postwar era and in many ways knitted the country together. For the first time perishable goods such as flowers, fish, vegetables, fruit, meat, and dairy products could be delivered economically across the nation. Eventually, medicines, pharmaceuticals, and organs for transplant were delivered within hours.

United's cargo system was continuously refined by the addition of new equipment and technologies. In 1954, United introduced RAF (Reserved Air Freight), a program that permitted shippers to reserve space on specific flights. Two years later, an epoch ended when, for the first time in United's history, cargo surpassed airmail as a source of revenue. In 1958, at Chicago's Midway Airport, United installed the industry's first significant mechanized freight-handling system. From 1966 through 1975, United operated 727QC (Quick Change) freighters between New York and Chicago. These planes could be converted from passenger to freight carriers in 30 minutes by removing the seats.

In 1973, United introduced its Air Freight Information System, the most advanced computerized freight monitoring system available in the nation at that time. AFIS enabled United to offer a priority service called First Freight for small packages. And at the same time, United was able to carry larger and larger loads. Where the size of the load was once limited to what would fit in the space left over after the mail was stowed, by the late 1970s each United freighter was carrying the cubic capacity of two railroad boxcars—up to 46 tons of payload.

United relied on an extensive interline system until 1997, partnering with overseas carriers to create an international freight service. Then it extended its system beyond U.S. borders, adding all-cargo flights across the Pacific.

By the beginning of the 21st century, United was flying more than 3 billion tons of cargo annually. Cargo operations had grown into a $900 million annual business, offering service to 102 domestic and 37 international airports in 27 countries and two territories. Through its interline system, United now delivers goods to a total of 170 destinations in 95 countries. Since 1998, the airline has spent more than $150 million to build new high-tech cargo facilities and enlarge and modernize existing facilities in major cities around the world.

In 1910 it took more than an hour to ship a bolt of silk 65 miles from Dayton to Columbus, Ohio. Before the end of the century, United's SameDay℠ service, in cooperation with NextJet, Inc., was offering a remarkable door-to-door U.S. delivery service for packages weighing up to 70 pounds. And United's Cargo Division Web site, www.UnitedCargo.com, allows customers to track their shipment throughout its journey.

The air cargo industry evolved from carrying the mail, as did United itself. Fittingly, no matter how much United's freight system has grown, mail even now accounts for 25 percent of all shipments. *W*

The Boeing 747 is so big that it has been said that it does not fly;
the earth merely drops out from under it.
—PAN AM CAPTAIN NED WILSON

THE JET AGE |

IN THE CLOSING DAYS OF WORLD WAR II, GERMANY UNLEASHED THE ME 262, THE WORLD'S FIRST JET-POWERED fighter. The aircraft arrived too late to effect the war, which was fortunate because it so outperformed every propeller plane extant that the twinjet Messerschmitt fighter could have ruled the skies of Europe. It wasn't long after the war's end that all the major world air forces preferred jet-powered fighters over propeller-driven planes, and the airlines eagerly followed.

United began investigating the potential of turbojet power after President Pat Patterson attended a 1947 presentation by Air Commodore Frank Whittle, the Royal Air Force engineer who developed the first jet engine for the Allies. Patterson was impressed by what he heard and immediately appointed a technical committee within United to learn everything there was to know about this remarkable engine. Ray Kelly, United's superintendent of technical development, went with two other executives to Europe to study jet engine technology in 1950. (Kelly was honored on his 100th birthday in 2001 by the American Institute of Aeronautics and Astronautics.) The committee gathered information from a variety of sources and sent pilots to U.S. Air Force training centers to gain firsthand experience in jet operation.

Some planners within the airline questioned the practicality and safety of mixing 500-plus mph jets with propliners operating at half that speed. To address the concerns, the committee created a "paper jet" airline in November 1952. Every day for a year, phantom jetliners took off from San Francisco and New York on imaginary flights to determine how they might impact the flow of the real DC-6 and DC-7 Mainliners churning along the airways that day. The flights were planned to operate at 30,000–40,000 feet and were subject to the actual weather and operational conditions that existed each day. In all, the paper jets made more than 600 trips before the exercise ended.

Donald Douglas (left), **the genius behind the DC-3, posed in 1959 with the first generation of his jetliner the DC-8. The medal above marked the 1967 debut of the Super DC-8. By 1961, United had the world's largest jet fleet.**

Satisfied that jets would mesh quite easily with their propeller-driven brethren, United began to work up the specifications for its dream plane. It went so far as to build a full-scale mockup of a jet fuselage within the San Francisco maintenance base. The mock interior was outfitted with passenger seats and galleys that cabin and ground crews used to learn how best to conduct meal services, baggage loading, and other day-to-day procedures.

By conducting such studies early on, United was able to conclude that the jetliner it needed was not the first one that became available—the British-built de Havilland Comet. The four-engine

In 1970, flight attendant Nancy Butscher dramatized the size of the new fanjet engine that powered the mammoth Boeing 747. Over the years, United photographers took many such photos to capture the ever-expanding scale and aspirations of aviation.

jetliner had begun international service with British Overseas Airways Corporation in 1952. And while it delivered many of the promised benefits of jet travel—500 mph cruise speeds at turbulence-free altitudes well above the weather—United's planners felt the Comet's 36-passenger cabin was too small and its 1,750-mile range too short. United decided to wait for the right airplane.

The wait wasn't long. By then Boeing was very familiar with producing large jets, having built the B-47 and the B-52 bombers for the U.S. Air Force. Boeing wanted to apply its expertise to the civilian market and gambled heavily on developing an all-new aircraft. The Boeing 707 began flying in 1954. United was interested.

Although Boeing clearly had taken the lead, Douglas Aircraft, then the most successful manufacturer of airliners, announced that it would also build a jetliner. It called its design the DC-8. United paid close attention to the new DC-8 as well as the 707. The two aircraft were remarkably similar. Both had four engines mounted on pylons hung below highly swept wings, and both would carry about the same number of passengers approximately the same distance.

Patterson ordered mockups to be built using the cabin dimensions of both models. The Boeing design was narrower by 3 inches, a noticeable difference. Patterson had a particular aversion to "sardine loading" of passengers, and he suggested that Boeing widen its aircraft (a request United would later make with the Boeing 777, for the same reason, in the early 1990s). But Boeing had already committed huge sums of money to the design, which was being adapted to serve the Air Force as the KC-135 aerial tanker. The 707 and KC-135 were supposed to share the same production line and tooling. Consequently, Boeing refused Patterson's suggestion.

And so even though the 707 prototype was flying and the Douglas design was merely in the planning stage, United chose the latter. In October 1955, Patterson signed a $175 million contract for 30 DC-8s, making United the first domestic airline to order jetliners. The first domestic U.S. airline to actually offer jet-powered service was Capital Airlines in 1955—which United acquired in 1961—with the British-built Vickers-Armstrong Viscount turboprop liner. United chose to wait for the newest turbojets, so it was a slight latecomer to the Jet Age—Pan Am, American, National, and TWA were all flying 707s months before United began DC-8 service late in 1959. But by 1961, the inflight magazine *Jetage Airlanes* was reporting that United had the "world's largest jet fleet." Ultimately, United operated 117 DC-8 Jet Mainliners, which it flew from 1959 to 1991.

As it turned out, other airlines shared Patterson's concern about the 707's dimensions, and Boeing decided to alter the cabin after all, making it 1 inch wider than the DC-8s. The 707 went on to achieve tremendous success, particularly among international operators. Boeing also made a lighter, shortened version of the 707 designed for domestic operations, which it designated the 720. That aircraft worked particularly well in United's system. Undoubtedly, both Boeing and Patterson felt a special sense of satisfaction when United ordered 720s in 1957, the first of 29 the airline put in service, all of them sized just as Patterson had originally requested.

In the late 1960s, United was in the thick of the industry's embrace of jumbo jets. Optimistic projections of growth in passenger volume and a desire for increased cabin comfort lent added appeal to the Boeing 747, DC-10, and the Boeing 767 (which United was the first to introduce, in 1984). At first, the jumbos flew just partially full on domestic routes. But they later provided the passenger capacity to fuel United's growth around the globe. ⦀

The 21st Century starts today.

Circular Fuselage and Lower Cabin Floor Combine For Amazing Headroom.

Today, United Airlines celebrates the first flight of our new 777. This is the plane that will lead all others into the future. How did it come to be? The first 777 is called "Working Together." That tells the story.

The 55,000 employee-owners of the world's largest airline had ideas. Our frequent flyers had ideas. And, of course, the designers at Boeing had ideas. Never before in the history of the airline industry have so many contributed so much.

The 777. Only on United. From Chicago, Denver, Washington, D.C., London, and Frankfurt. Soon Paris, Amsterdam and Newark.

It's obvious we don't just work here. Come fly our friendly skies.

 **UNITED AIRLINES**

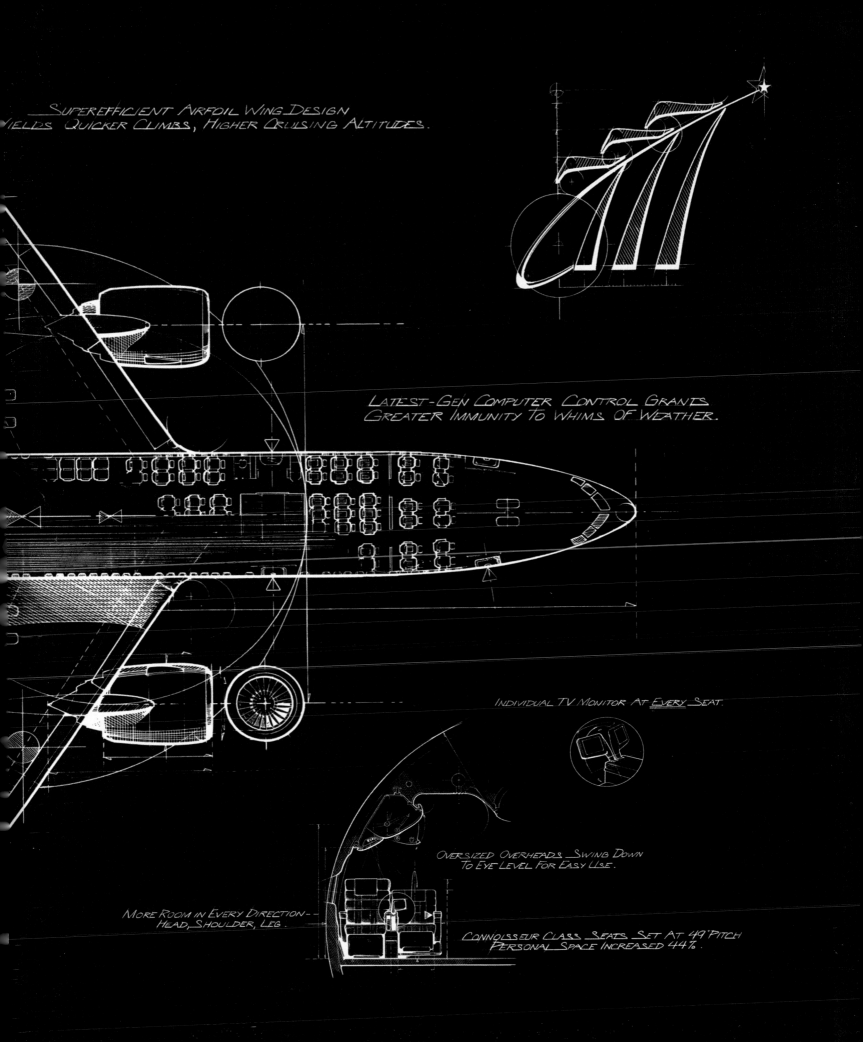

SUPEREFFICIENT AIRFOIL WING DESIGN
YIELDS QUICKER CLIMBS, HIGHER CRUISING ALTITUDES.

LATEST-GEN COMPUTER CONTROL GRANTS
GREATER IMMUNITY TO WHIMS OF WEATHER.

INDIVIDUAL TV MONITOR AT EVERY SEAT.

OVERSIZED OVERHEADS SWING DOWN
TO EYE LEVEL FOR EASY USE.

MORE ROOM IN EVERY DIRECTION-
HEAD, SHOULDER, LEG.

CONNOISSEUR CLASS SEATS SET AT 49"PITCH
PERSONAL SPACE INCREASED 44%.

A marvel of the digital age, the 777's computers translate its pilots' control inputs by signalling actuators to move the flaps, ailerons, and elevators accordingly. This workhorse for the 21st century is Boeing's first "fly-by-wire" jetliner.

were too small for maintenance workers wearing heavy gloves during winter operations at places like Chicago's O'Hare. Boeing made the buttons larger.

The United team successfully championed a move to outfit the cockpit with the most advanced electronic instruments available. But even though the aircraft's highly computerized systems would have permitted the use of a small joystick to manipulate the flight controls, United and Boeing chose to retain the pilots' traditional control columns for the sake of procedural uniformity.

The effort to make the aircraft easy and convenient to operate continued inside the cabin. Tapping the experience of United employees who work within the fuselage—from the people who clean the planes to the flight attendants who see to the safety and satisfaction of customers—the United team advised on everything from galley placement and seating design to baggage stowage.

Stephen Wolf, a former United chairman and CEO, examined mockup cabins of the 777 and two of its rival widebodies, the Airbus A330 and McDonnell Douglas MD-11, all fine designs. However, when the 6-foot-7-inch executive rose from the Airbus seat, he smacked his head on the overhead luggage bin. Boeing's designers had anticipated such unpleasant encounters and equipped the 777 with a new kind of pivoting overhead bin that offered more headroom than the traditional drop-down bins featured on the A330. The new bins also had a larger volume to accommodate more readily the carry-on luggage that so often choked bins of earlier designs.

United's McKinzie also recalls that "from Day One we pushed for wider seat bottoms" on the 777. After all, the airplane was to fly a long, long way and, to assure maximum comfort on flights spanning multiple time zones, United wanted as much room as possible for every passenger. Specifically, it wanted coach seats wider than the 18-inch seats on the DC-10, giving 777 passengers the widest coach seats in the business. But it also wanted to retain the DC-10's nine-abreast coach layout.

To accomplish that, Boeing added five inches to the 777's girth. That expansion cut the airplane's range by 30 miles, but it gave each coach passenger an extra half inch. That makes the 777's coach seats an inch and a half wider than the coach seats on the 747—additional width that becomes more appreciated with every hour spent occupying it.

United was so satisfied with the new aircraft that in October 1990 it became the 777's launch customer, signing for 34 of them with an option on another 34. That bold commitment, part of a $22 billion order for Boeing widebodies, was the key to the 777 program's go-ahead.

In the development process that followed, the aircraft, its systems and subsystems underwent excruciating testing to win certification. One phase included a demonstration in which a single aircraft would take off, cruise, and land 1,000 times, simulating two years of airline operation in a period of months. United flight crews and technicians participated in that 1,000-cycle test, operating and maintaining the aircraft on the airline's routes. The tests went so well that when the FAA certified the aircraft in May 1995, the agency permitted it to travel transoceanic routes that were as much as three hours' flying time from an airport, even when operating on only one engine. No airplane had ever received such an endorsement at the start of service.

Critical to that approval, of course, were the engines. They had to be reliable, durable, and powerful—each one had to be capable of sustaining flight of the half a million-pound aircraft. After evaluating all contenders, United chose the Pratt & Whitney 4077, thus continuing a partnership begun so many years earlier when Bill Boeing equipped his Model 40 mail planes with the air-cooled Wasp engine. Once again, Pratt & Whitney's trademark flying eagle helped give wing to a breakthrough Boeing aircraft.

United launched 777 service on June 7, 1995, and today operates 50 of the remarkable twin-engine giants on routes throughout the world.

Thanks to Boeing's high design goals, its solicitation and adaptation of input from United and other carriers, and United's early and substantial commitment to the project, the 777 has not only set new standards for efficiency and safety but has proved far more comfortable for passengers than any of its predecessors.

Although United's 777s embody the most advanced design, systems, and materials in commercial aviation today, they also represent a tradition and a role that date back to the airline's very beginning. United began life as an aviation pioneer, and it continues that early commitment to advance aviation, making it safer, more efficient, more reliable, and more comfortable for all involved, customers and competitors alike. The 777 does all that, just as United anticipated one day in 1990 when it committed to help bring the jet to life.

123

From unprecedented airline involvement to enhanced passenger comfort, the Triple 7 has launched aviation into the 21st century.

SELLING THE SKY

If that plane leaves the ground and you're not with him, you'll regret it.
Maybe not today, maybe not tomorrow, but soon, and for the rest of your life.
–RICK BLAINE, IN THE 1942 MOVIE *CASABLANCA*

UNITED AT YOUR SERVICE | 133

THE FIRST AIRPLANE PASSENGER CLIMBED CAREFULLY THROUGH AN ARRAY OF RODS AND WIRES INTO THE SMALL SEAT next to Wilbur Wright and placed his feet firmly on a small bar. After Wright's *Flyer* lifted off, the passenger held on for dear life. With flights measured in minutes and total feet traveled, inflight service was limited to some sensible advice—"Hold onto your hat"—and inflight entertainment was the ride of a lifetime.

Most U.S. airlines were content to profitably transport the mail, so the passenger experience didn't improve much for the next two decades. Then airlines began competing for passengers. Most were flying similar airplanes, and fares over the same routes were regulated by the government. The major difference was the quality of the service, ranging from meals to entertainment.

After Boeing Air Transport began serving food on flights in 1927, dinner consisted of a ham-and-cheese sandwich and an apple, or lukewarm creamed chicken in a Thermos and rolls, which the copilot usually handed to the passengers as they boarded. Pre-brewed coffee was kept warm in jugs heated by the plane's electrical system.

With the introduction of the trimotor Boeing 80 in 1929, fried chicken, a bag of potato chips, and an apple were served on almost every flight. A year later, Boeing Air Transport revolutionized the aviation industry by hiring eight young women to tend to passengers. "Imagine the tremendous effect it would have on the traveling public," wrote San Francisco traffic manager Steve Stimpson when he proposed the idea to company management. "Also imagine the value they would be to us not only in the neater and nicer method of serving food but looking out for the passenger's welfare." With the hiring of these first stewardesses the business of inflight service changed significantly. Pleasing the customer had become second in importance only to flight safety.

Pleasing passengers has been a United priority since the days of the DC-3 sleeper (left) **and Mainliner service** (top). **United's expanding late-1940s service to Hawai'i** (preceding pages) **did portend hanau—the birth of something new.**

Among stewardesses' many tasks, serving meals was one of the most important. However, that did not extend to serving alcoholic beverages. Prohibition was still the law of the land. Stewardesses were cautioned to warn passengers about sipping from flasks or "cough syrup" bottles. Even after the end of Prohibition, United did not serve alcoholic beverages until 1956. Pat Patterson long contended that he did not want to turn stewardesses into "flying barmaids." When United was forced to offer alcoholic beverages to meet competition, he insisted, "We will not sell drinks, but rather serve them as hospitality," and he set a two-drink limit.

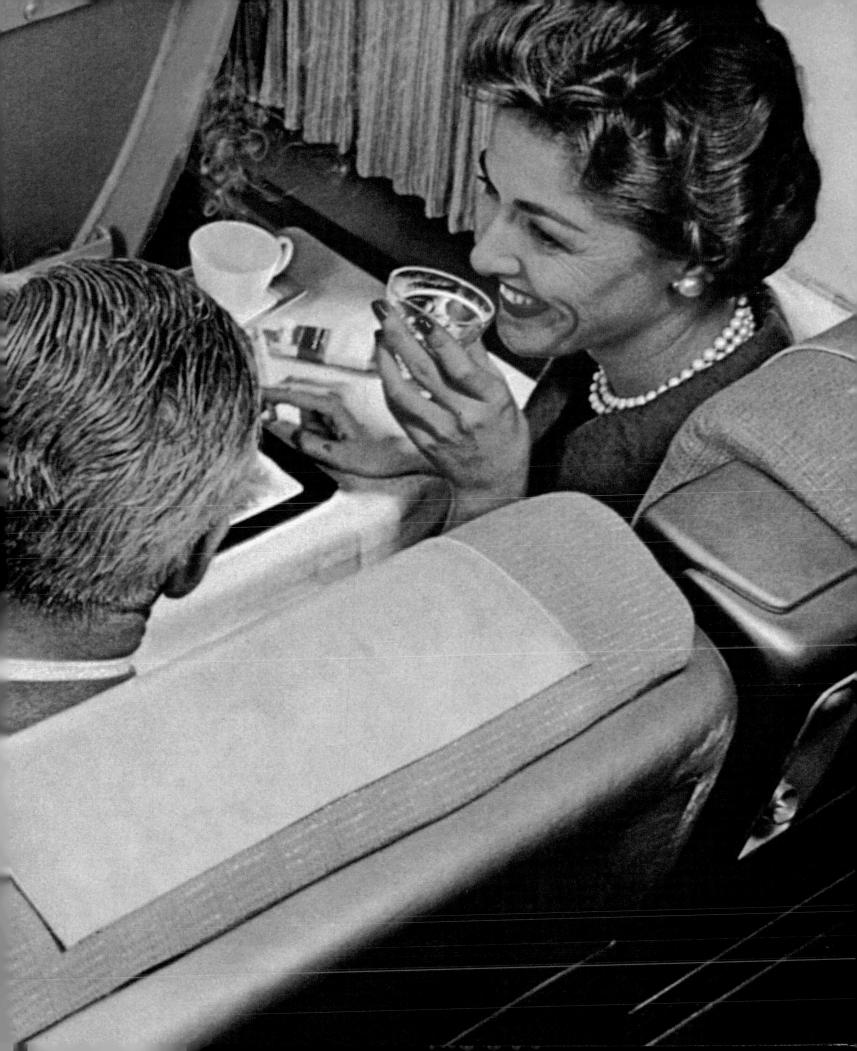

United's 1936 launch of the first flight kitchen put quality on the menu. Holiday whimsy was added in the late 1940s. DC-8 ads (preceding pages) *proclaimed, "The best of the jets is here."*

Modern food service started in 1933 when the Boeing 247 went into widespread use on United routes. The 247's larger cabin allowed stewardesses to serve complete meals for the first time. China was eventually replaced by paper plates because it tended to break during the inevitable rough landings.

The airlines quickly discovered that serving good food required considerably more preparation than just reheating. Air and cabin pressure cause many foods to taste different, and some foods could not be served at all. Sponge cake and lemon meringue pie, for example, collapsed at high altitudes. Fried eggs turned green at the edges. Even some beverages proved sensitive to the lower air pressure: Other airlines discovered that certain wines lose much of their taste in flight. One drink urged on passengers was carrot juice—its taste was unchanged by altitude.

Food had become an important weapon in the competition for passengers. To help win the battle, United spent $5,000 in 1936 to open the industry's first flight kitchen in Oakland, California. Three days later the first hot meals—a choice of fried chicken or scrambled eggs—were served aboard a DC-3. The meals were kept hot in an electrically heated compartment designed by United's engineers, and each had been wrapped in heavy paper to provide insulation, then packed in a papier-mâché box that doubled as a lap tray. In the early 1950s the arrival of the now-ubiquitous individual seat tray led to the demise of that kind of packaging.

Preparing the meals was only half the job; delivering them hot to passengers in flight was the other. In the late 1930s, while United was playing a leading role in the design of the four-engine DC-4, airline personnel suggested the galley be moved from its traditional location at the front of the plane to a spot near the rear door. The resulting galley was more spacious, which made it easier for ground crews to stock meals, and for the first time allowed the installation of equipment for actually heating food in flight. By 1946 United was able to offer a wide selection of meals on its DC-4s. Modern airliners still use convection or conduction ovens to heat food because microwaves can interfere with communications equipment.

Besides creating a flight kitchen, United formally organized its Passenger Service Department to meet the growing needs and desires of air travelers in 1936. The following year, United set itself apart with Skylounge. Pat Patterson had taken his cue from the railroads. Just as the railroads offered first-class and coach service in different cars, Patterson felt airlines should offer different levels of service in different planes. The Skylounge was commercial aviation's first extra-fare plane—in effect launching the concept of first-class air travel. On several new DC-3s flying the New York–Chicago route, United replaced the normal 21 seats with 14

United offered customers the industry's earliest inflight magazines—publications that have helped define the modern travel magazine.

In the 1930s, inflight food was memorable whether it was a full breakfast (right) **after a night stretched out in a Douglas DC-3 sleeper berth or dinner aboard a Skylounge** (far right).

deluxe swivel seats with ottoman-style footrests, providing a new level of comfort and spaciousness. The airline charged passengers on the Skylounge an extra $2 for this luxury service. And what it lost in seven full fares it gained in publicity.

In those early years the most exciting inflight entertainment was the flight itself. One passenger suggested that United build planes with windows in the cabin floor to permit better viewing. If passengers grew bored with the map and playing cards, there was a selection of newspapers and magazines purchased by stewardesses who were reimbursed by the airline.

Inflight magazines debuted on United in 1936 with a magazine called *Airlanes,* which was distributed on several airlines around the world. Launched in United's hometown, Chicago, it set the standard for nearly 30 years, and its approach characterized the genre for longer than that. It carried monthly spreads of photos—"People You Know" and later "On the Go"—of celebrities waving from the top of the boarding stairs (pages 164-167). The mission was to popularize flight, with everything from photographic "Earthward Glances" at stunning scenes out the window (a small town-looking Manhattan pre-Empire State Building) to first-person tales about the avoidable pain of a drive across the desert before air conditioning—"Next Time, We'll Go By Plane."

At their best, these magazines were among the first modern travel magazines. A generation before *Condé Nast Traveler* and *National Geographic Traveler* hit newsstands, United's *Mainliner Traveler* (launched in 1947) became the first inflight magazine published for a single airline. Articles were written by civic leaders and often focused on airline destinations. But the travel industry was being invented, and interesting features found their way into print. Some covered the growing use of rental cars and incentive travel. Others promoted the ski industry emerging as once-isolated U.S. resorts became increasingly accessible by air. In 1957 *Mainliner* became the title of United's new inflight magazine, the first general interest magazine published by a U.S. airline and "one more example of service in the Mainliner manner."

In 1982 United retired the last vestige of its venerable "Mainliner" name. The new *United: The Magazine of the Friendly Skies* replaced *Mainliner* magazine and reflected the airline's growth far beyond the Main Line route across the United States. The magazine became *Vis à Vis* in 1987. Then in 1992, with an increasingly global route system, United launched *Hemispheres,* a magazine intended to break the mold of the company-newsletter style of inflight publications. Produced by custom publisher Pace Communications, *Hemispheres* became the most award-winning inflight publication in the industry, netting accolades against the biggest consumer magazines and being repeatedly named the best U.S. travel magazine by the Society of American Travel Writers.

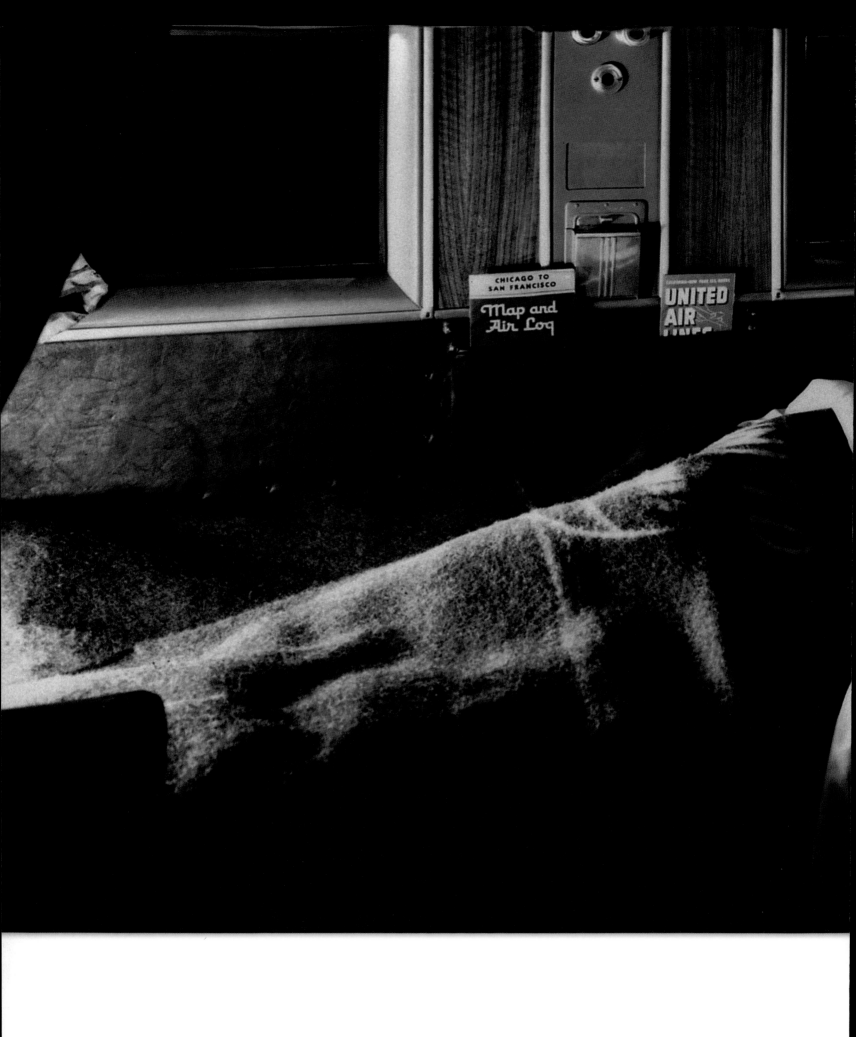

The pleasure of an airborne bed aboard the DC-3 Mainliners of the 1930s (above) *returned in 1999 with United's remarkable First Suite.*

United has offered special services for a wide range of customers—from infants and toddlers to newlyweds, wives, and car buyers— even businessmen who wanted a steak and a cigar with the guys. This brochure touted amenities for young mothers (right).

When *Airlanes* magazine first arrived in the 1930s, commercial aviation was still competing with the railroads. To keep pace with competition both on the tracks and in the air, United converted some DC-3s into sleepers. "Goodnight New York ... Good Morning California," boasted ads for this service. The berths resembled those on trains, but United's passengers had to be awakened before each landing to keep their ears from popping. The popular sleeper flights ended at the beginning of World War II when United handed over much of its fleet to the military.

In April 1940, United introduced the concept of coach service on flights between Los Angeles and San Francisco. For the first time, passengers would have the option of paying a reduced fare and receiving minimal service on more-crowded, older, and slower planes. All-coach flights proved very successful before being curtailed, like sleeper flights, at the beginning of World War II when civilian use of airlines gave way to military missions.

The introduction of coach class was only one of many different promotions used to attract passengers who might otherwise be reluctant to fly. Even before creating reduced-fare flights in 1940, United offered male passengers the opportunity to "take your wife free" as a way to fill empty seats while convincing women that flying was safe and fun. In 1946, United introduced "Nurseryliner" flights between L.A. and San Francisco, leaving every morning at 10 a.m. Ads promised mothers, "You'll find bottle coolers and warmers, books and games, baby kits... The only thing you'll need is baby's own individual formula."

One of the airline industry's earliest promotions continues today at United. In 1929, Transcontinental Air Transport, Inc. joined with the Pennsylvania Railroad to offer transcontinental service. United still promotes "the adventure of rail travel even if you don't have the luxury of time." Its Amtrak Air Rail packages permit travelers to go one way by rail and the other by plane, all at one fare with up to three stops on the rail leg. In the 1930s United offered connections to the French oceanliner *Normandie* and Air France, the French national airline. A similar inducement came about in 1949 when United arranged cost-saving "Fly to the Factory" plans with major automobile manufacturers. Buyers purchased their new cars from local dealers and then flew to the assembly plant to pick them up and drive home. The money saved on freight and handling more than compensated for the cost of the flight and related travel expenses.

For several years after the war, Patterson refused to go back to offering coach service because he believed it was "first-class business you took away from yourself." But as competitors' reduced-fare services attracted a rapidly growing number of passengers, Patterson had no choice. He gave in, but rather than squeezing passengers into the cabin "like sardines," United installed only 44 seats on coach flights as opposed to the competitors' 66. When other airlines protested to the Civil Aeronautics Board that this was unfair competition, Patterson agreed to install an additional 11 seats, which still gave United the roomiest coach flights in the industry. Even into the Jet Age, Patterson still believed that making different fares available on the same flight was a mistake. In 1963 he experimented with One-Class Service on jetliners between San Francisco and Chicago, charging slightly more than regular coach fares. That approach proved so successful that United quickly added coast-to-coast One-Class Service. But other airlines competed by lowering their own first-class fares over the same routes to a few dollars more than United's price, effectively ending Patterson's one-class experiment.

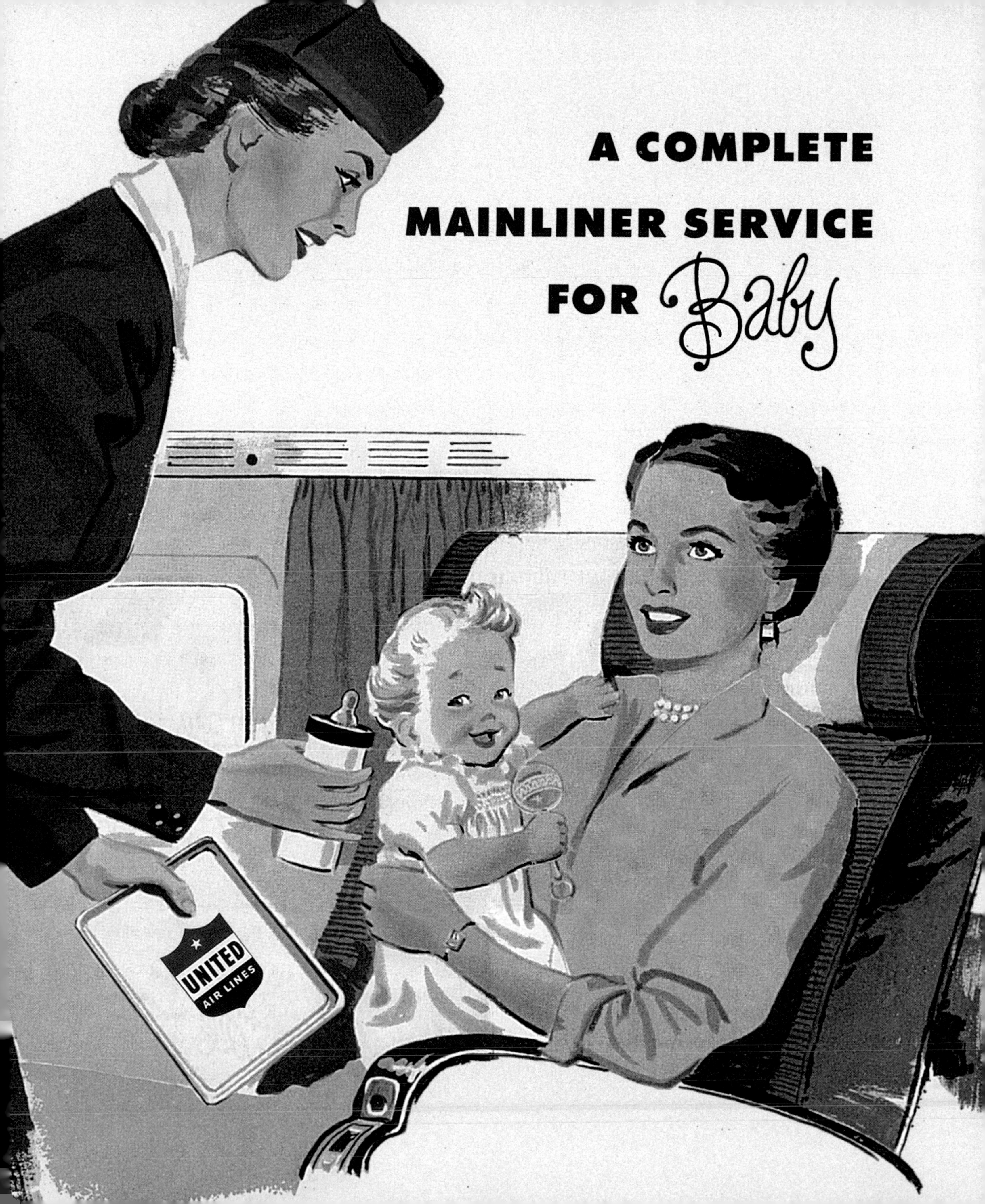
A COMPLETE
MAINLINER SERVICE
FOR Baby
UNITED
AIR LINES

146

By the mid-1950s the days of cold, wax paper-wrapped fried chicken were long gone. United's single flight kitchen had evolved into a systemwide network. Each was supervised by a bona fide European chef, an unprecedented step that launched a culinary tradition. The phrase "Mainliner service" had begun appearing in ads before World War II, and by now "Mainliner" meant more than just the planes that plied the Main Line. It had become a standard of excellence.

A monthly recipe from United chefs, whose resumés included the best U.S. restaurants, and features on Hawaiian cuisine were a 1950s highlight of the inflight magazine. For "25 cents in coin" you could mail order "Favorite Recipes of Mainliner Chefs."

In a reprise of the "take your wife free" campaign of the 1930s, United advised "Take Me Along" in the late 1960s. In that promotion, ads pictured a housewife asking her husband to "take me along," to which he responded, "I love you little cutie, but the office is my duty." In fact, as the general populace accepted flying as the most efficient way to travel for pleasure as well as business, husbands began taking their wives along in large numbers.

But not on all flights. In 1953 United had inaugurated a daily men-only executive flight between Chicago and New York designed to attract the hard-working "executive" flying home to greet "the little woman." On the flight the men took off their shoes and ties and relaxed, while lovely stewardesses gave them complimentary slippers, cigars, and stamps, as well as gifts like cuff links, letter openers, golf balls, and cigarette lighters. Then the weary businessmen enjoyed a hearty steak dinner. The success of the promotion prompted United to add a second plane to the New York–Chicago trip and start executive flights between Los Angeles and San Francisco.

A little-known skirmish in the "war between the sexes" was fought when a female executive was not allowed aboard the flight and filed a formal complaint with the Civil Aeronautics Board. After 10,500 trips the service ended in 1970.

In 1955 TWA began providing different classes of service, separated only by a thin curtain, on the same flight. United followed a year later. But Patterson continued looking for ways to promote United's more-luxurious, though more-expensive first-class service. In 1956 the airline began serving Kansas City for the first time in 22 years. To celebrate and promote this new route, United flew a group of Kansas City citizens to San Francisco, treating them to the kind of royal treatment long known as "rolling out the red carpet." The trip was so well-received that United decided to offer similar treatment to all its first-class passengers, and Red Carpet Service, the ultimate in luxury, was born in September 1956 on a select group of flights.

For a time, ground crews literally rolled out a red carpet between metal stanchions and chains for these passengers, although more-durable red rubber rugs soon replaced plush. On the plane, specific seats were reserved, which was unusual at that time, and passengers received special treatment, from space to stretch out to memorable meals. Red Carpet Service remains a hallmark of United's worldwide network of airport Red Carpet membership clubs.

Throughout its history, United has promoted reduced-fare programs to increase passenger traffic. In the 1930s, passengers booking roundtrip passage in advance received a 10 percent discount. Years later there were Family Fares, and a program called "Take the DC-8 to the 50th State" boosted United's new jet service to Hawai'i.

One of United's most successful programs promoted the entire aviation industry rather than only its own service. In 1959,

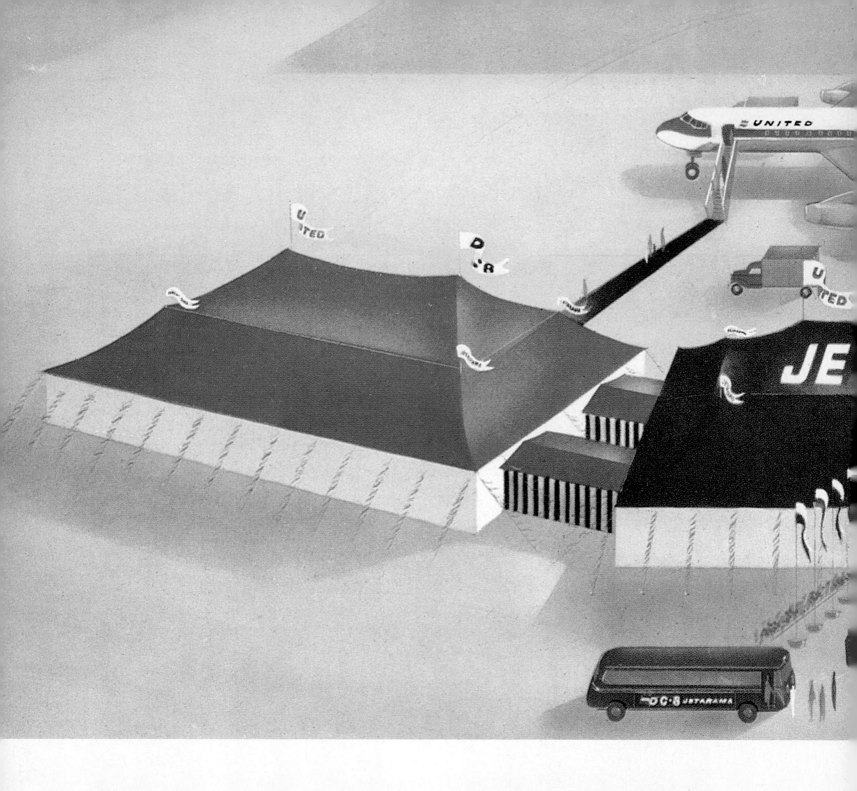

DC-8 JETARAMA

Watch f

...'s great three-ring jet age fair introducing the DC-8 Jet Mainliner to your city

United's traveling exhibition entitled "Jetarama" helped build excitement—and reassure passengers—in 1959, the dawn of the Jet Age.

Jetarama featured mock-ups of the DC-8 cabin (right) *as well as cutaways of its four Pratt & Whitney JT3C-6 engines, but the main draw was the DC-8 parked outside. United benefited from the publicity, but the real winner was air travel.*

concerned that the traveling public might be reluctant to make the transition from propeller-driven planes to the new jets, United sent "The Greatest Airline Show on Earth," called Jetarama, on a 12-city national tour.

To introduce United's new DC-8 Mainliners, Jetarama toured United's system for more than a year, receiving more than a million visitors. To introduce potential passengers to the Jet Age, the show used one DC-8 and three huge tents. The Dependability Pavilion stressed the safety of jet-powered flight, the Safety Pavilion showed how crews were being trained to fly jets, and the Extra Care Pavilion emphasized the additional interior comforts. By the time visitors toured the actual airplane, they were familiar with jet-powered flight and the magic of modern aviation, whether or not they were in the market for air travel.

As the industry grew, food remained a focus of United's service. In 1971 United launched its first menus inspired by a celebrity chef—"Trader Vic" Bergeron. The popular Pacific-influenced meals and tropical drinks from the international chain of restaurants were served on transcontinental and Mainland-Hawai'i routes—and symbolized by logos and even figurines of the elflike Hawaiian little people called *menehunes*. Chairman/CEO Edward E. Carlson cooked up the innovation with Bergeron, creating a flamboyant departure from airline dining standards of the time.

In 1994 United returned to restaurant-themed menus in association with Doc Cheng's at the Raffles Hotel in Singapore. In 1999, the Ritz-Carltons in Hong Kong and Singapore were inspiring the dishes. The Celebrity Chef program again added the recipes of culinary stars to United routes starting in 1997 with Sheila Lukins' American regional cuisine. Then came dishes by Jacques Pépin. Specialties by Martin Yan and Sam Choy featured flavors from Asia and Hawai'i. Great restaurant chefs, among them Chicago's Charlie Trotter and Norman Van Aiken in Miami, lent a U.S. flair, as did selections from eateries participating in the Taste of Chicago Food Festival. United routinely offers special Chicago treats like Eli's cheesecake. Starbucks coffee became the airline's regular brew in 1995, further fueling United's commitment to fine cuisine.

Eventually 16 flight kitchens turned out 80 million meals annually—everything from filet mignon to mahi-mahi, accompanied by a range of drinks from spring water to fine wines. In 1990 United Airlines ranked among the largest 25 restaurant chains in the nation. In 1993, following the industry trend, United sold most of its flight kitchens to Dobbs International Services/Gate Gourmet, the largest catering company in the airline industry. While the recipes and menus are still created and tested by United's own chefs in the airline's test kitchens, the actual food preparation is done to United's specifications by caterers—one example of the partner relationships that mark onboard service and the airline industry in general.

In addition to the various regular meals created by the airline's "culinary design team," United's customers can pre-order dozens of meals to fit an amazing array of special medical, religious, or dietary needs. Even specific age groups get special consideration. In 2001 United went from McDonald's Friendly Skies Meals to Junior Wings meals that come with a kid's magazine.

As new entertainment and communication technologies developed, they were adapted to the special needs of the airline industry. The first experimental radio-telephone calls from commercial airliners were made in the 1930s. In 1947 United was the first airline to install radio telephones for inflight use by passengers. A Bell Telephone representative reportedly became the first

Once jets took to the skies, inflight entertainment came into its own. Cloud gazing was replaced with audio and video programming. United aircraft have featured movie premieres, the first inflight television sitcoms, and even the debut of a new album.

person to book a hotel room from midair when poor weather caused him to miss a connection. Airfone telephone service, with inflight access to e-mail, came much later. An early United exclusive had become a convenience accessible from every row. United would be among the first to offer passengers electrical outlets for laptop computers.

The first real attempt to provide inflight visual entertainment can be traced back at least to 1929, when newsreels and cartoons were shown on National Air Transport's new 18-passenger Curtiss Condors. Experiments with inflight closed-circuit television began in the '30s, and United was the first to demonstrate the potential of inflight television in 1951 when it showed a college football game on an ordinary TV set fastened to a table.

A major form of inflight entertainment got its start in 1957 when a bored motion-picture exhibitor flying to California looked around the cabin and was thrilled at what he saw—a captive audience. Airlines were a new and potentially huge market for films. After considerable technical problems were overcome, including a lack of space and weight limitations, movies were introduced by TWA in 1961, and by 1964 United was showing movies on transcontinental and Hawai'i-bound flights. United's first film was an inflight first—a world premiere. The MGM film *Quick Before It Melts* didn't hit theaters until the following year. Another film premiered in 2001. Jackie Chan's *Rush Hour 2*, which featured a United jet, debuted on the Hong Kong route. Initially only one film was offered on each flight, but by the 1990s passengers could pick from among 14 films in English and six in a second language, all available on video screens at their seats. The screens also offered a broad range of new inflight television programs exclusive to United, ranging from episodes of top-rated sitcoms to news and documentaries.

In addition to television, United passengers today can choose from as many as 19 audio channels, providing everything from classical to country music; regional entertainment for audiences from Asia to Europe, India to South America; and special programming. In 1999 an audio first for United found passengers enjoying Garth Brooks' new album before its general release. To enhance inflight programming, United was an early adopter of the noise reduction headset, a marvel that electronically neutralizes the whoosh of the airplane, canceling out everything but the music—or sleep.

In 2000, for the second time, United won the World Airline Entertainment Association's award for the world's best inflight entertainment—an honor based on the combined quality of the print, video, and audio components of the airline's inflight entertainment. United is the only U.S. carrier to have won it.

As passenger loads rose dramatically at the end of the 20th century, the airline responded first with United Economy Plus℠, adding 5 inches of space between rows in the front of the coach section of domestic flights in the spring of 2000. Economy Plus proved so popular that international Economy Plus was added in 2001, and that same year a similar expansion of space was implemented throughout United Business on three-class international aircraft. Seats could recline to a nearly flat 150 degrees. United was also the first U.S. carrier to bring back beds. United First Suite, a first-class seat that converts to a lie-flat bed, was introduced in 1999, and within two years, most of United's fleet of three-class international aircraft had First Suite.

When Pat Patterson listed his Rule of Five to guide the fledgling airline, passenger comfort was second only to safety. Throughout its first 75 years United has endeavored to go the extra step for customer safety and satisfaction. *✈*

If I were a United publicist, I would take the position that Hawai'i
is the state that United built. United service played a key role in statehood.
Today we look at United as our pioneer airline.
—U.S. SENATOR DANIEL K. INOUYE

HAWAIIAN LOVE AFFAIR | 157

IN THE 1920S AND '30S PAN AMERICAN AIRWAYS WAS RENOWNED FOR PIONEERING TRANSOCEANIC ROUTES LINKING the United States to the rest of the world. It began modestly by flying between Florida and Cuba, but by 1940 its then-famous Clipper flying boats coursed east to Europe, south through the Caribbean to Central and South America, and west, island-hopping from Hawai'i to the Philippines and beyond. It was the United States' flag carrier to the world.

That unique and enviable status ended after the surprise air attack on Pearl Harbor in December 1941 brought the United States into World War II. Suddenly all of the country's resources were needed to counter foes on two fronts, and the U.S. War Department conscripted airliners outright for transport and cargo duties, and contracted for scheduled supply and training services.

By late 1942, dedicated United aircraft and crews were crisscrossing the Pacific in military service from the States to Australia via Hawai'i—an 8,269-mile transpacific route—with pilots who a year earlier had been flying strictly domestic overland routes.

Based in part upon this extraordinary experience as well as the conviction that increased air service would permit Hawai'i to become a major travel destination, United in 1944 submitted an application to the Civil Aeronautics Board (CAB) proposing to serve the Islands from San Francisco and Los Angeles. The CAB, which then controlled all routes and fares, granted the request in 1946, thus ending what had been a Pan Am monopoly.

On May 1, 1947, a United DC-6 Mainliner 300 lifted off from San Francisco and banked west out to sea bound for Honolulu, then the longest over-water commercial airline route on earth. That flight marked the start of a transformation. Until then the

Pat Patterson was welcomed to Hawai'i in the '50s (left). United promoted Hawai'i with posters (above) and the 1970 campaign "Our Little Corner of the World." The Boeing Stratocruiser graced many ads (preceding pages and 161).

Hawaiian Islands had been a vacation spot for only the well-to-do, but United's frequent flights and low fares attracted the middle class to the Islands by the thousands. That popularity increased even more when flights from Los Angeles were added in 1950. The airline recorded its 10,000th California-to-Hawai'i crossing the following year and, more significant, passed Pan Am in volume of traffic between the Mainland and Hawai'i. United was on its way to becoming the Main Line to the Islands.

In 1960 United was carrying 60 percent of all air passengers from California to this newest member of the United States. And thanks to the 550–600 mph cruising speed of the newly inaugurated DC-8 jets, passengers escaping a wintry Chicago could be on the beach in Waikiki just 10 hours later.

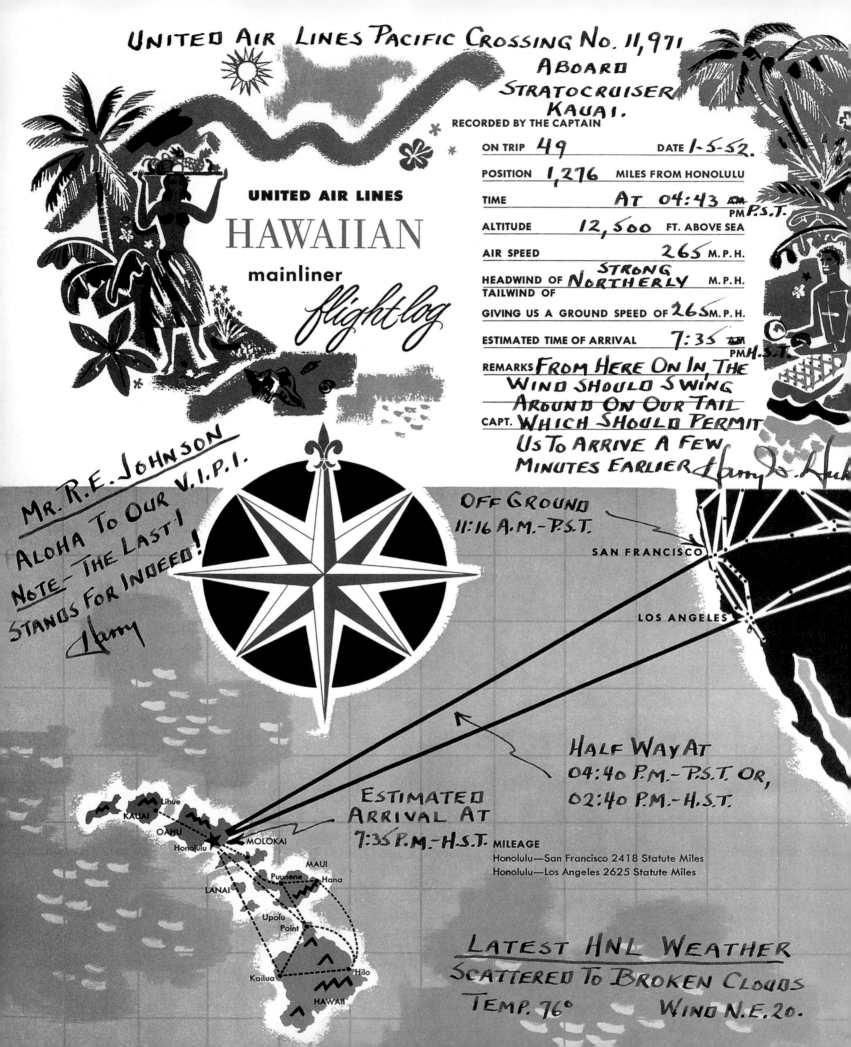

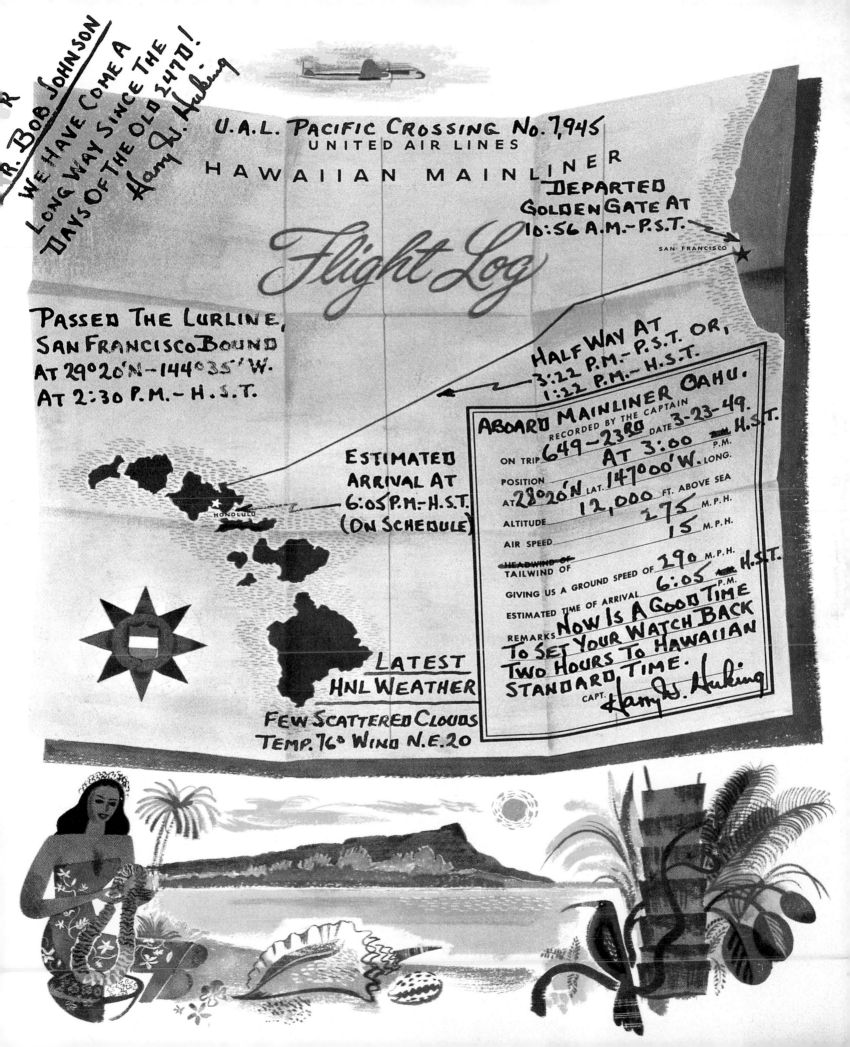

U.A.L. PACIFIC CROSSING No. 7,945
UNITED AIR LINES
HAWAIIAN MAINLINER

Flight Log

MR. BOB JOHNSON
WE HAVE COME A
LONG WAY SINCE THE
DAYS OF THE OLD 247D!
Harry W. Huking

DEPARTED
GOLDEN GATE AT
10:56 A.M. — P.S.T.

SAN FRANCISCO

PASSED THE LURLINE,
SAN FRANCISCO BOUND
AT 29°20'N — 144°35'W.
AT 2:30 P.M. — H.S.T.

HALF WAY AT
3:22 P.M. — P.S.T. OR,
1:22 P.M. — H.S.T.

ESTIMATED
ARRIVAL AT
6:05 P.M. — H.S.T.
(ON SCHEDULE)

HONOLULU

ABOARD MAINLINER OAHU.
RECORDED BY THE CAPTAIN

ON TRIP 649 – 23RD   DATE 3-23-49.
AT 3:00 P.M. H.S.T.

POSITION
AT 28°20'N LAT. 147°00'W. LONG.

ALTITUDE 12,000 FT. ABOVE SEA

AIR SPEED 275 M.P.H.

HEADWIND OF
TAILWIND OF 15 M.P.H.

GIVING US A GROUND SPEED OF 290 M.P.H.

ESTIMATED TIME OF ARRIVAL 6:05 P.M. H.S.T.

REMARKS NOW IS A GOOD TIME
TO SET YOUR WATCH BACK
TWO HOURS TO HAWAIIAN
STANDARD TIME.
CAPT. Harry W. Huking

LATEST
HNL WEATHER

FEW SCATTERED CLOUDS
TEMP. 76° WIND N.E. 20

United fanfare—such as this 1972 menehune *figurine—helped build Hawaiian tourism. Flight logs* (preceding pages) *went to first-class passengers. Captain and former airmail pilot Harry Huking penned two for United's R.E. Johnson. An enticing 1950s menu from United's Hawai'i-based chef* (following pages).

United did all it could to coax people into the air by promoting paradise, sometimes with comical results. The airline often sent groups of travel agents to Hawai'i on familiarization trips. On one such trip, the United sales executive acting as host knew a lot about salesmanship but not much about Hawai'i.

As soon as the engines were cut in Honolulu, ramp crews rolled up a stairway while rolling out a red carpet, the symbol of United's Red Carpet Service. A welcoming group of Hawaiian musicians, hula dancers, local United managers, media representatives, and an official of the Hawai'i Visitors Bureau clustered below. As United's host led his group to the tarmac, the Visitors Bureau representative stuck out his hand and boomed, "Aloha, from Hawai'i."

"Kowalski, from Chicago," came the United host's enthusiastic reply.

By 1969 there were three Mainland airlines serving the Hawaiian market, but United was carrying the most passengers. Those flights accounted for $19 million in profit for the airline. That fact did not escape notice by envious competitors or the CAB, which that year approved service to Hawai'i by five more domestic lines. The initial results of that decision were disastrous; the sudden overcapacity meant red ink all around. United alone lost $17 million in 1970, the same year it received new 747s ordered four years earlier to serve Hawaiian routes.

Although those circumstances severely tested United, the quality, convenience, and frequency of the airline's service ultimately won out, reaffirming its position as the leading carrier to the Islands.

Today, excluding traffic to Mainland hub airports, Hawai'i is United's second-largest single destination, accounting for 3.2 million passengers a year. The airline serves the Aloha State with flights between the Mainland and O'ahu, Maui, Kaua'i, and the Big Island of Hawai'i. United 747s also carry sun-seekers daily from Tokyo.

United's service has meant more than easy access to a premier vacation spot. "It has played a key role in developing the Hawai'i we know today," says Hawai'i's first U.S. congressman, later longtime senator, Daniel K. Inouye. "United was the air carrier that stood by Hawai'i and stayed with Hawai'i, from the mid-'40s on." In 1997, on the 50th anniversary of United's Island service, the senate of the state of Hawai'i honored United for a half-century of "commitment to the state and its people."

For millions of people, the wonder of the United States' Pacific island paradise starts thousands of miles away when they step aboard a United airliner. ///

CUSTOM-DESIGNED CABIN
View from forward cabin toward galley and aft cabin. With room for 100 passengers, United limited seats to 55 for greater personal comfort!

FAMOUS "SNACK BAR" BUFFET
A delicious bountiful spread of your favorite foods allays healthy appetites before arrival on day flights.

BIG, SQUARE "PICTURE WINDOWS"
Another great feature of the World's Finest Stratocruiser! Windows are wide, double-paned, add greatly to the atmosphere of spaciousness . . . insure a better view!

PRIVATE STATEROOM
Offers secluded accommodations for three persons on day flights. Has private clothes and baggage closet, rest-room, spacious divan, table and lamp, and big windows. Berths for two persons.

pacious **IS THE WORD FOR**

UNITED'S BOEING-BUILT,

LUXURIOUS, TWIN-DECK

MAINLINER *Stratocruiser*

LOWER-DECK HAWAIIAN LOUNGE
Nearly sixteen feet long and over six feet high. Windows provide unobstructed scenic views. Fourteen passengers can relax in comfort on its cushioned, horseshoe-shaped divan. Fresh, modern color.

MEAL SERVICE
Mid-cabin location of MAINLINER *Stratocruiser's* electric galley equipment permits fast, efficient preparation and serving of complete hot meals and the tempting hors d'oeuvres and cold specials featured on United's popular "Snack Bar" buffet.

FORWARD BERTH COMPARTMENT
Seats for eight persons make up into four luxurious berths on night flights. Berths wider than conventional twin-bed; have foam-rubber mattresses. Curtains insure complete privacy.

COMPLETE REST-ROOM FACILITIES
Separate, attractive lounges. Women's lounge has lavatory, two vanity tables with settees and large mirrors. Men's lounge features two mirror-covered walls and excellent lighting for speedy shaving.

SPECIFICATIONS

Overall length	110 ft. 4 in.	Seating capacity	55 passengers
Overall height	38 ft. 3 in.	Normal operating altitude	15,000 to 25,000 ft.
Wing span	141 ft. 3 in.	Cruising speed (25,000 ft.)	300-340 mph
Total horsepower	14,000	Gasoline capacity	7,790 gal.

—9½ hrs. BETWEEN THE MAINLAND AND *Hawaii . . .*

No matter what month of the year you find yourself daydreaming about the warm Hawaiian sunshine, the flower-scented trade winds, and lazy afternoons on palm-fringed beaches—you can be sure these lovely islands are just as you're imagining them!

Of course, it's a lot more fun to put yourself right in that picture by spending a couple of never-to-be-forgotten weeks in the "Paradise of the Pacific," finding out what there is about Hawaii that makes you want to return again and again.

Now that United's MAINLINER *Stratocruisers* make the Islands more readily accessible than ever, it's like having a tropical garden in your own back yard! You can actually leave from many United terminals (in 300-mile-an-hour DC-6 Mainliner 300s to California) and arrive in Aloha-land the same day!

Each of the major islands of Hawaii has its own distinctive scenic appeal. You'll want to see them all. Excellent inter-island air service, provided by Hawaiian Airlines and Trans-Pacific Airlines, will whisk you from Honolulu to the outer island of your choice in a matter of minutes.

OAHU "Gathering Place"
Stroll along Honolulu's fascinating streets and enjoy the cosmopolitan atmosphere of a city where the intermingling of Oriental and Caucasian culture is everywhere in evidence. Ride to the summit of Mount Tantalus for the sweeping view of Honolulu and the harbor. Shop for souvenirs in modern, well-stocked stores in Waikiki and Honolulu. Enjoy glass-bottom boat rides over mysterious coral gardens at Kaneohe and Haleiwa. See the magnificent valley view from the Nuuanu Pali . . . drive round the Island through vast sugar cane and pineapple fields, past Diamond Head Crater, Kahana Bay, Pearl Harbor, and scores of other sights you'll always remember.

HAWAII "The Big Island"
On the largest of the Hawaiian Islands you'll find some of

nature's most imposing scenery. See Hawaii National Park, spectacular Kilauea Crater, towering Mauna Loa, dense fern jungles and weird lava flows. Other must-see features on Hawaii are snow-capped 13,825-foot Mauna Kea, Rainbow Falls near Hilo (second largest Hawaiian city), and the dreamy Kona Coast with its tranquil native villages and historic sites.

MAUI "The Valley Isle"
Great bamboo forests, sculptured cliffs, and astonishing plants like the *ape-ape*—with its yard-wide leaves, are just a few of the sights that delight Maui visitors. Also on this scenic island is the world's largest inactive crater, vast Haleakala ("House of the Sun"), and Iao Valley, the "Yosemite of the Pacific" and famed Hana.

KAUAI "The Garden Isle"
Sculptured Waimea Canyon is the most celebrated of the many scenic features of the "Garden Isle." Its tremendous depth and brilliant-hued walls remind one of Arizona's Grand Canyon. Other attractions include the Barking Sands, the beautiful Na Pali Cliffs, and the legendary caves at Haena.

...iew from Nuuanu Pali, near Honolulu.

Famous beaches like Waikiki offer grand water fun.

Air-Sea Holiday: Go one way air, one way Matson Lurline.

Brilliant Torch Ginger is typical Island flower.

Scenic grounds of Hotel Hana-Maui on Maui isle.

MARC A. GRUGIER

Honolulu

HONOLULU

After several years of culinary training at Bordeaux, France, Chef Grugier prepared cuisine for the clientele of many world-famous hotels—the Continental in Paris, the Savoy in London, the Waldorf-Astoria, Sherry-Netherlands, and Essex House in New York, and the Roney-Plaza in Miami. He also was employed at famous restaurants, such as Sherry's, and by the French Line. The savory dishes he now plans for United reflect an intimate knowledge of Continental and American cookery.

SEATTLE -TACOMA

PORTLAND

SAN FRANCISCO

OAKLAND

LOS ANGELES

SAN DIEGO

Mainliner MENU

This menu prepared in United Air Lines Flight Kitchen at Honolulu, Marc A. Grugier, Chef.

Salad Bowl Excelsior
Roquefort Chive Dressing
Wafers

Roast Boned Squab Veronique
Peas à la Menthe
Asparagus Mornay

Poppy Seed Roll

Fresh Blueberry French Tartelette

Coffee   Tea   Milk
Dinner Mint

The Pinot Chardonnay served with this menu
and the Champagne "Aloha Toast" are from
the Paul Masson Vineyards, Saratoga, California.

U. S. Department of Agriculture Regulations prohibit
use of certain fruits and vegetables in natural or raw
state in menus on all flights from the Territory of
Hawaii to the Mainland.

Frank Sinatra

Dwight D. Eisenhower

John F. Kennedy and Richard Nixon

CELEBRITY STATUS / *They were everywhere—on the front pages of the world's newspapers, in United's earliest inflight magazines—celebrities waving out at the nonflying world from the open doorways of early airliners. These blatant public relations photos became the icons of the Age of Flight.* ▰ *You knew flying was safe—even glamorous—when Marilyn Monroe, Bob Hope, Joe DiMaggio, Nat King Cole, and the Marx Brothers seemed so at home in the air and on the steps leading down to the tarmac.* ▰ *To this day, one of the perks of being a flight attendant is frequent sightings of the rich and famous. Even after Air Force One swept U.S. presidents into airborne seclusion, a historic, decades-long list of office seekers took to the campaign trail on scheduled flights or leased planes. United was, and still is, there with them.*

Will Rogers

Julie Andrews

Nat King Cole

Katharine Hepburn

Jimmy Carter

Amelia Earhart

FLYING ON LEADERSHIP 80 / By Elizabeth Kaye McCall / *During the 1980 U.S. presidential election campaign, both the president, Jimmy Carter, and his opponent, Ronald Reagan, chartered United jets. I was privileged to be among the flight attendants picked to serve on LeaderShip 80—the United stretch 727 chartered as Reagan's campaign plane. Like most United flight attendants, I'd encountered celebrities onboard before, but even celebspotting during the 1930s golden age surely paled in comparison.* ⊎ *Besides Reagan and his wife, Nancy, an entourage of VIPs, future White House staffers, veteran news correspondents, celebrities, and dignitaries surfaced all the time. Henry Kissinger came aboard. I'll never forget Bob Hope—a United "million-miler" who is easily the subject of more photos with United planes and personnel than any other celebrity. We were photographed comparing noses that angled in decidedly different directions (upper right).* ⊎ *Traveling together week after week on LeaderShip 80, we not only got to know our famous passengers, we saw in Reagan what the country would come to love over the years—a fresh informality and genuineness. On Halloween we dressed in costumes. Photos of the future president, smiling and surrounded by a jockey, nun, and Keystone cop, subsequently made the wire services and our personal scrapbooks.* ⊎ *The crew was included in many off-plane events— Reagan's debate with Jimmy Carter, a Frank Sinatra performance at the Waldorf Astoria. We had our share of limousine rides.* ⊎ *For the final campaign flight to Reagan's hometown, Los Angeles, we donned Western clothes and cowboy hats. The next night at the Century Plaza Hotel victory party, the crew who'd traveled on LeaderShip 80 saw candidate Ronald Reagan elected president.* ⊎ *The nonstop camaraderie made that campaign the experience of a lifetime. Willie Nelson's hit song "On the Road Again" always came over the speaker system as the plane climbed out. As the wheels came up, all eyes looked to the aisle—and Nancy Reagan invariably bowled an orange down the length of the plane.*

Marilyn Monroe

The Marx Brothers

"Stewardess, will you let me know if any celebrities get on the plane?"

DICK SHAW

Rocky Marciano

Joe DiMaggio

*I recall vividly the conclusion of the agency's presentation. They threw back a
curtain over a big blackboard and on it was written "Fly the Friendly Skies." Obviously
they thought this was the greatest thing since sliced bread and were disappointed
that I didn't get up and cheer. But at that moment it just didn't hit me.*
—GEORGE KECK, UNITED AIR LINES PRESIDENT, 1963–1970

FLY THE FRIENDLY SKIES

ADVERTISING IS A CORPORATION'S PUBLIC VOICE, THE METHOD IT USES TO TELL THE WORLD WHAT IT DOES AND HOW it does it. But it also reflects the popular culture, and over United's eight decades of flight, its advertising helped invent a clientele for an industry even as the industry itself was being invented. That effort can be traced back to the early 1920s when Walter Varney sent typed letters to potential customers informing them, "On April 6 at 6 a.m. ... [we] will inaugurate the greatest mail service ever offered to the people of the Great Northwest.... Air Mail will mean a savings of ninety hours between the Northwest and the East.... We feel sure you will grasp the opportunity to 'Use Air Mail.' We need your *letters* and your *cooperation.*"

Early on, it was indeed the public's cooperation that was needed—people weren't used to putting their mail, much less themselves on airplanes. Before advertising could sell tickets it had to sell a dream, inspire a need, create a market.

In effect, United's first slogan was "Use Air Mail," and it was plastered on mailboxes, billboards, barns, and government mail trucks. Boeing Air Transport, which urged newspaper and magazine readers to "Mail by Air," made an auspicious though inconspicuous announcement in 1927. "On July 27 [Boeing] took over the contract for the airmail route between Chicago and San Francisco. The 25 Boeing airplanes to be used on this route will accommodate two passengers in addition to the mail and express." That may have been United's earliest passenger ad.

In addition to placing print ads in newspapers and magazines, the airlines distributed penny post cards featuring tranquil scenes to promote destinations—the earliest instances of the still-important role airlines play in creating and sustaining the travel industry. They also did tie-in advertising with suppliers like Pratt & Whitney, which boasted that its engines enabled passengers to fly "Over the Rockies With the Modern Pony Express." The effect was to give the travel industry a lift over the rough overland road.

In 1930, a year after the formation of the United Aircraft & Transport Corporation, the airline hired its first professional advertising agency, J. Walter Thompson. To counter the general belief that flying in winter was particularly dangerous, as well as to create a positive image for the new corporation, United built its first national magazine advertising campaign for *The Saturday Evening Post, The New Yorker,* and *Collier's* around the single theme "The Main Street of the Skyways." And to further acquaint viewers with the excitement and safety of air travel, the airline

**"Come Fly With Me,"
sang Frank Sinatra in a
1969 United ad campaign
that tweaked the lyrics
of his popular song of
the same name. "Let's
fly," he sang, "let's fly
today. If I advise those
Friendly Skies, would you
take a holiday?"**

United Air Lines is the

only airline linking the East,

the Middle West, all major

Pacific Coast cities and Hawaii.

Wherever you travel,

fly United's Main Line Airway—

truly the Nation's

No. 1 Coast-to-Coast Airline.

UNITED
AIR LINES

MORE VACAT
YOU WANT IT.

UNITED'S MAIN LINE AIRWAY
Linking All Major Eastern and Pacific Coast
Cities with America's Finest Vacation Lands
UNITED AIR LINES
CONNECTING AIR LINES

Spend extra days in Colorado, Yellowstone, Boulde
yon, California, Yosemite, Pacific Northwest, Alask
Washington, New York or New England. Go one

★ TWO WEEKS IS PLENTY OF TIME for
the vacation you've always dreamed of—if you
fly United's Main Line!

Just think. You spend only a few *hours* en-
route, instead of *days* . . . get to your vaca-
tionland *overnight* even if it's 3,000 miles away!

Flying United is easy on your budget, too.
Complimentary meals, no "extras!" Costs are
comparable to good surface transportation.
United's is the *mid-continent* route. Thus

United can offer yo
twice as much at no
turn another, on

This year, don't
drum vacation! Go
office or a good trav
a glorious time you
and how little it wo
cious days, by flyi
Main Line Airway!

UNITED'S
MAIN LINE AIR

TIME WHERE
ou fly United's
n Line airway!

Fly in the new-type
1938 MAINLINERS

—the fastest, quietest, most powerful large transports in the country!

★ United's magnificent new fleet of Mainliners can fly 227 miles an hour—"loaf along" at 205 m.p.h. using only 60% of horsepower!

15% quieter, too—in spite of increased speed and power, the new Mainliner cabins are so quiet that you can talk as quietly and easily as in your own living room.

Their new-type, more powerful twin Wasp engines and new "full-feathering" propellers—the first to be installed on a fleet of airliners—give a marked increase in flying efficiency at United's higher and smoother prescribed flying levels...remarkable take-off, climb and cruising performance.

Can-
cago,
ther.

ou see
way, re-
ticket!
a hum-
Lines
t what
eeks—
ny pre-
o-coast

What airline has an expert in <u>every</u> job?

It's United Air Lines proud of serving you better in <u>every</u> way!

A while ago someone asked one of our Mainliner cabin cleaners, "Why are you so particular about getting every speck? Do you think the passengers will notice the difference?"

The cabin cleaner was surprised by the question. "You bet they will," he replied. "My passengers like to have their airplane clean, same as their homes. *They expect it on United Air Lines.*"

The remark illustrated the kind of pride you'd find in every position on United Air Lines. All of the 18,000 United people feel the same way about "Service in the Mainliner Manner."

This service makes even routine air travel suddenly become refreshingly different. Superb dependability, comfort, courtesy, convenience and speed add up to a trip that is, from beginning to end, flight at its finest! For reservations call or write United or an Authorized Travel Agent.

UNITED AIR LINES

Copr. 1955, United Air Lines

*There's a **difference** when you travel in the Mainliner® Manner*

A decade after the birth of commercial aviation, United's ads touted the convenience and employee expertise of the Main Line Airway.

172

Dazzling service was the theme for 1967's ad "Miss Butterfingers" (right).
Flight attendant Sheri Woodruff "couldn't even balance a cup of coffee two
weeks ago." In 1952, value and convenience were the message (far right).

produced and distributed a travel film, *Across America in 27 Hours.* It was shown in theaters and at private gatherings throughout the nation in 1932.

Most of United's advertising for the remainder of the 1930s was designed to inform the public about the airline's equipment and service as well as reassure people that flying was safe. An ad headlined "Which Air Line Shall I Choose?" emphasized United's experience: "In nearly ten years of flying this line has covered 80 million miles"; its service: "Experienced travelers praise United's personalized service and unfailing courtesy"; and its commitment to safety: "United's pilots are thoroughly experienced, with thousands of hours of flying to the credit of every man." To address the fact that other airlines were at that time using faster airplanes, the ad pointed out that "Mere speed is never allowed to interfere with passenger comfort."

The number of miles safely flown by the airline and its pilots became a staple of advertising and an impressive measure of United's "world record" experience in the air. Through the years, ads touted the total miles flown by the airline as well as by individual pilots. Eventually, the numbers became mind-boggling. Today, even a conservative measurement of United's total miles flown would be almost incomprehensible—unless it was phrased in terms of interplanetary space travel.

In the late 1930s the theme "The Main Line Airway" appeared for the first time, accompanied by a new slogan to remind readers that United was "More than a route ... a standard of service." "Now Insurance Companies Recognize the New Safety of Air Travel," boasted one ad, pointing out that "Leading insurance companies have reduced the cost of air travel insurance to the same 'per mile' rate as for rail travel—a tribute to the dependability of air travel today." This ad also stated that "Every United pilot has rigid orders to fly at least ½ mile above the ground on every flight." Another 1930s ad, "You Can't Judge Flying Weather by Looking Out Your Office Window," said that "United gets up-to-the-minute weather data from four different sources," and assured customers that the salaries of United pilots had recently been guaranteed, meaning that "United pays them for their judgment in not starting a trip." And "Your Mainliner Is A Brand-New Ship ... every 500 flying hours" told of the dedication of United's "veteran corps of the most expert airplane mechanics to be found anywhere." The ads established in the public mind that United's safety and reliability depend as much on skilled professionals working on the ground and behind the scenes as on the stewardesses and pilots that customers see on their flights.

By February 1939, N.W. Ayer, which had replaced J. Walter Thompson as United's advertising agency, created ads emphasizing

New Record!

This year people are flying United Air Lines at the rate
of around a quarter of a million passengers monthly — a new winter
record. While other forms of travel have been increasing
in cost, United's fares have stayed within about 4% of the 1941
level. Yet your United Mainliner ticket represents a far
greater value than it did then, with almost twice the speed . . .
larger, more spacious, more luxurious planes . . . improved
schedule dependability . . . finer meals . . . and direct service to
more cities (83 in all today) on the only airline that
links the East and Midwest with all the Pacific Coast and Hawaii.
Call or write United Air Lines or an Authorized Travel
Agent for your *best* travel buy — reservations on
The Nation's Number 1 Coast-to-Coast Airline.

PASSENGERS · MAIL · EXPRESS · FREIGHT · AIR PARCEL POST

UNITED AIR LINES

Presents its Great New

This month United Air Lines marks on
the truly significant events in the prog
of air transportation. It is our privileg
present the first transport plane built s
the war — the 4-engine Mainliner 300.

It is fitting that upon the wings of this
tinguished plane should rest the honor of u
ing in a new day of flying. Combining the l
in speed, operating efficiency and travel
fort, it is the most advanced airliner in ser

Further, the scientific new *pressurized c*
maintains atmosphere at *comfort-level* no

MAINLIN

how high in the smooth upper air the giant ~~pla~~ne may fly. Changes in pressure are no ~~lon~~ger noticeable.

~~T~~he interior appointments of this Douglas ~~D~~C-6 type Mainliner 300 set a new note in travel ~~lu~~xury. The spacious cabin, with its two sep-~~ara~~te compartments, is so large it could easily ~~ac~~commodate 72 passengers. But United has ~~lim~~ited the seats to 52. Thus each passenger ~~ha~~s more room for personal comfort.

~~I~~ncluded in the outstanding features of the ~~Ma~~inliner 300 are constant air conditioning, soft, indirect lighting, comfortable reclining chairs which are individually adjustable, delicious table-served meals and lounges for men and women.

To date there has been nothing like the Mainliner 300 in the sky. Winging its way over United's straight, strategic Main Line Airway, its cruising speed of more than 300 miles an hour brings cities served by this route closer to each other than ever before. And with the finer, faster, extra-fare Mainliner 300s, "service in the Mainliner manner" takes on new meaning.

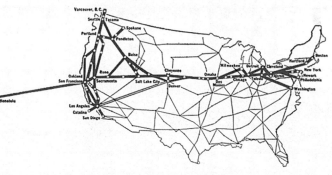

ER *300*

THE DOUGLAS DC-6

SAMPLE MAINLINER 300 FLIGHT TIMES

San Francisco—New York	10 hrs.
Chicago—New York	2¾ hrs.
Honolulu—San Francisco	8⅔ hrs.
Seattle—San Francisco	3 hrs.
Portland—Los Angeles	4½ hrs.

Extra fare: one-half cent per mile.

See your nearest United office or travel agent.

PASSENGERS · MAIL · EXPRESS · FREIGHT

The growing importance of women in the workplace was reflected in United advertisements during the war (right)*. This one invited executive women—and their daughters—aloft. 1947 ads featured the inspiring technology of postwar travel* (preceding pages)*.*

176

that United was "The Nation's FIRST Airline" and listing many of the airline's achievements in the development of commercial aviation, among them: "First to complete 25,000 Coast-to-Coast flights. First to fly 135,000,000 miles. First to use important aids such as airport localizer beams, automatic mixture control, static suppressor, and recording barograph."

In 1940, United became the first airline to sponsor a regular program on a major radio network—a news commentary show on the Mutual network hosted by a popular military pilot named Boake Carter.

As commercial aviation became accepted as a safe and efficient means of transportation, United began emphasizing the competitive advantage of its transcontinental and Pacific coastal routes under the banner "The Business Route of the Nation." One ad showed a pony express rider with a plane high above and said to the reader, "*Clip-clop.* Can you hear him, traveler? *Clippity-clop, clip-clop.* Dusty hoofs on a sun-baked plain. Listen, traveler-by-air, as you soar along United's Main Line Airway, the Business Route of the Nation. History is riding below you!"

History was riding above, too—"at three miles a minute," the ad gushed. That incredible speed was a far cry from the snail's pace of mail planes just a decade earlier, much less the pony express that had ridden below on what was indeed much the same route as the Main Line. United's employee newsletter reported when pilots set speed records on their routes; decades later, today's travelers take 10 miles a minute for granted.

United's advertising also touted the Mainliner crews, often with the implicit sexism of the era. One such ad, titled "Two Men and a Girl," showed two rakish pilots and a stewardess standing proudly in front of their DC-3. The captain and first officer were listed first by title and qualifications, while the stewardess's bio started with "charming" and her height and weight came before the fact that she was a registered nurse.

Throughout World War II, the airline reminded the public that it was continuing mail, freight, and passenger service, and a growing number of those home-front passengers were professional women. "Women Department Store Executives are among our most enthusiastic regular passengers," one ad titled "First Flight" explained beneath a picture of a mother and stuffed animal—toting daughter striding out to their Mainliner. United gently invited women into the air—"A woman's first 100 seconds in the air are apt to be an important experience ... This is it ... this at last is FLYING. Perspective lines vanish so not a trace of the dizziness or dread of high places she may have anticipated is present. No sense of restriction or of grimy 'travel fatigue' invades the bright airy luxury of the cabin. Because women take to wings so happily—Mainliners will be designed for serving YOU."

During the fall of 1942, United instituted a new campaign titled "The Age of Flight." Headlines like "The Age of Flight in the Free Tomorrow for which we Fight" predicted an exciting future for commercial aviation once the war was over.

In explaining United's advertising policy, the airline's newsletter promised employees, "It has been and will continue to be our policy to observe truth in advertising." While that sounds like a claim easily made, in some postwar advertising United dealt with real problems. An ad headlined "To those who fly United Air Lines," read "While service aloft continues to merit approval, United's handling of its passengers—on the ground—is not what it should be." That ad explained the source of United's difficulty

in meeting postwar demands and the steps it had taken to solve the problem.

After the war, ads touted leisure travel. "Short Cut to Summertime" promised that "In just a few enjoyable hours, you'll be starting on that welcome healthful tan" in places like Hawai'i—just $135 from San Francisco.

After a DC-6 caught fire and crashed in Bryce Canyon, Utah, United grounded its fleet of 34 DC-6s. An ad headlined "The Facts behind United's withdrawal of DC-6 Flights" candidly discussed the situation, outlining what the airline was doing to protect its passengers and "insure the complete operating safety and dependability of the DC-6." The frankness of those ads established a tone and an approach that has become a hallmark of how the airline addresses its customers when the news isn't good. In the summer of 2000, CEO Jim Goodwin followed suit when he apologized for summer flight delays in print and television ads.

United ads frequently compared fares with earlier times and showed how the price of travel was declining. A 1940 ad pointed out that coast-to-coast fares had decreased from $400 to $150 since the 1920s. By the 1950s, once again the message was economy, as well as safety and reliability. "When Dollars Count" reminded businessmen that "The hours you'll save on United Mainliners will mean cash in your pocket ... You'll spend your time there, not getting there," and noted that "On United Mainliners delicious meals are included in the cost of your ticket ... When you reach your destination four or five times more quickly, you don't have those 'incidental expenses' that run into so much money." "An Old Fashioned Dollar's Worth" compared airfares with those of a decade earlier and showed that some airline fares were actually cheaper than comparable railroad fares. That kind of comparison may no longer be the advertising message, but a New York-to-San Francisco fare of $150 in 1940 is $1,800 in year 2000 dollars—far more than the current price of a coach ticket on the same route.

The year 1952 signaled United's entry into television on major shows like Edward R. Murrow's *See It Now*, the drama series *Studio One*, and *Quiz Kids*. Most print advertising through the '50s was straightforward, once more promoting service: "Smoother, More Dependable Flights with the World's Largest Radar Fleet"; price: "New speed, New comfort, superb service ... the Ultimate in Low Cost Travel"; and modern equipment: "United Expands Jet Fleet." To promote the new Custom Coach DC-7 service, ads promised "Extra Care at the Regular Fare." "On Schedule With A Flight Plan You Gave Us 25 Years Ago" reminded travelers that "The art of flying has been advanced ... United has become self-sufficient ... Gets no air mail subsidy."

By the early 1960s, commercial aviation was universally accepted as a safe and reliable form of transportation. So once again

The world, and United's advertising, have changed. As routes crossed oceans, ads began to cross cultures, too. This ad is from 2001.

"Fly the Friendly Skies" may be the best-known campaign in United's history, but Gershwin's "Rhapsody in Blue" has also become synonymous with the airline (right). *"United We Fly" celebrated reaching the 50,000 employee mark in 1977.*

180

United's advertising focused on its superior routes and jet fleet, reminding passengers that the airline was "Far Ahead" of competitors in getting them where they wanted to go comfortably and on time, and would remain so in the future.

In 1965, after 26 years with N.W. Ayer, United hired a new advertising agency, Leo Burnett. That year marked the introduction of the airline industry's longest-running marketing message and one of the most successful and enduring campaigns in advertising history. Rather than another campaign focusing on specific aspects of the airline, United wanted to create an identity, an indelible image about the airline in the passenger's mind. So Burnett created the "Fly the Friendly Skies" campaign. Everybody was flying by then, and "Fly the Friendly Skies" was intended to emphasize that United wanted and welcomed passengers' business.

Other memorable campaigns followed. In 1967, to persuade men traveling on business to bring along their wives, United built a tremendously successful campaign around the bouncy song *Take Me Along*, in which a woman suggests, "Take me along, if ya love-a me." But slightly more than a decade later, that particular message had changed drastically. Women were entering the workplace in record numbers. The "Lady Boss" campaign was designed to appeal to female business travelers, one of the fastest-growing segments of the aviation industry. In 1969, the airline was humming another tune, as Frank Sinatra sang the theme song of the "Come Fly With Me" ad. Through the years many other celebrities figured in campaigns. Among the people who did voice-overs for TV spots were Burgess Meredith, Robert Duval, Gene Hackman, and Liam Neeson. Through the 1980s and into the '90s, United's advertising reinforced the "Friendly Skies" message to make people feel more secure about flying in general and flying United in particular. It was replete with beautiful pictures of destinations from Hollywood to New York City. In 1987, Leo Burnett used composer George Gershwin's majestic *Rhapsody in Blue* as background music for numerous commercials, and it quickly became synonymous with United.

In the 1980s, United expanded into the Pacific and then to Europe and Latin America in the early '90s, and its advertising reflected the airline's international flavor. While Leo Burnett's campaigns won numerous awards, in 1996 United ended its 31-year relationship with the agency. Young and Rubicam was hired to create international advertising, and the Minneapolis-based agency Fallon McElligott was awarded the domestic account. United was spending more than $100 million annually on advertising.

The objectives of the two agencies were quite different. United was the leading domestic airline but was not well-known in other countries. In many places it was competing directly against national flag carriers. So in 26 countries and 15 languages, Y&R's ads had the job of introducing United. In an ad titled "Boy on a Hill," for example, a young boy is running around holding a cardboard airplane high in the air, when from behind the hill a United jumbo jet appears and fills the sky.

After the introductory ads appeared, a second campaign attempted to explain why passengers outside the United States should fly United. A 1998 spot in this "One More Good Reason Why People Who Fly for a Living Fly United" campaign simply pictured an airplane with a huge surgical mask over its nose, as the message revealed that United was the first airline to install HEPA-filters—which scrub out 99.97 percent of bacteria from the cabin ventilation system—throughout its entire fleet. A companion ad emphasized that United offered "The freshest on-board air in the air. Put it together with the most widebodies, our

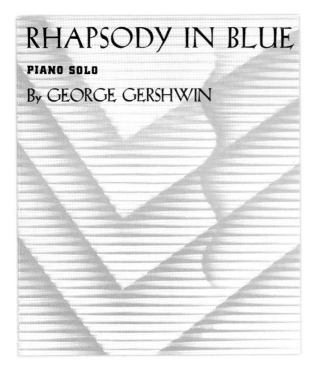

new business seat, and over 250 worldwide destinations, and you'll understand why people who fly for a living fly United."

The critically acclaimed but controversial domestic campaign called "Rising" was a cutting-edge TV version of United's 1940s print ads, which simply dealt with the reality that problems existed and the airline was taking steps to solve them. "Training Room," for example, featured a group of unhappy people who waited impatiently as a clock loudly ticked away. Finally a man entered the room and asked if everyone was tired of waiting. The group agreed unanimously and loudly. The camera then revealed that every person in the room was a United employee, and the man told them, "Hang on to that feeling the next time a frustrated customer comes to you with a problem. Make it your responsibility to fix the problem. Act like you own the place ... 'cause, you know, you do."

The "Rising" campaign had its detractors. Many people believed that it only served to remind passengers how frustrating flying can be, while some United employees felt that the ads were blaming them for industrywide problems. The campaign was replaced in 1999 by "Gatherings," which attempted to recapture the warm feeling conveyed by the original "Friendly Skies" campaign. One ad simply pictured people meeting in cities throughout the world, in town squares and plazas and courtyards, as an announcer explained, "Humans are a social bunch. That's why we fly to more places than anyone else. Because it's important for the human race to stay United." And with that emphasis on the global market, United in 2001 consolidated its advertising with one agency, Fallon Worldwide, who would manage the airline's brand all over the world.

Another ad in that campaign might have just as easily run 75 years ago, when the first Varney, Boeing, Pacific and National Air Transport planes hedge-hopped across pastures, laying the foundation for today's global airline. The ad pictured a person bicycling along a forest path. "Life is a journey," said the announcer. "Think of United as the road to the next village."

In 75 years, the Main Line of the pioneers had become as familiar as the road to the next town. *W*

THIS PLANE CARRIED THE STARS AND
STRIPES ACROSS THE FINISHING
LINE IN THE WORLD'S
GREATEST AIR RACE
LONDON
AIR LINES

UNITED AIR LINES

The Wright brothers created the single greatest cultural force since the invention of writing. The airplane became the first World Wide Web, bringing people, languages and values together. —BILL GATES, CEO, MICROSOFT CORPORATION

EXTENDING THE MAIN LINE | 185

UNITED GREW TO BECOME ONE OF THE WORLD'S LARGEST AIRLINES BY FOLLOWING THE UNUSUAL DICTATE OF STAYING close to home—to the United States. That policy gave United the opportunity to concentrate on technical developments, customer service, and marketing strategies—ingredients that facilitated its move into the international arena during the 1990s.

When the Roosevelt administration canceled commercial airmail contracts in 1934, many airline officials were banished from the industry, among them United Aircraft & Transport's president, Philip G. Johnson. Pat Patterson, who had been president under Johnson of the four predecessor carriers of United Air Lines, was outraged by the treatment meted out to his former boss. One of Patterson's first actions after Johnson's departure was to file suit against the federal government to clear Johnson's name. That litigation, which was ultimately decided in United's favor, went on for nine years and was a source of continuing irritation to the Roosevelt administration. Not surprisingly, United's applications to the federal government for route extensions and feeder-line acquisitions were denied during that period and for a long time thereafter. As a result, United's route structure remained largely unchanged until World War II. Meanwhile, other carriers had found favor in Washington, DC, and kept expanding until United lost its distinction as the country's largest carrier.

Though stymied by the government, United was looking for ways to expand. In 1940, United experimented with an "equipment interchange" agreement with Western Airlines. This sharing of flights was an innovative precursor of code-sharing agreements among airlines, an area where United would later lead the way. The two airlines ran a daily Chicago–Los Angeles sleeper flight via Salt Lake City with each airline's crew operating the flight over its own airline's route. At the time, the arrangement was said to be similar to the way Pullman sleeper cars were handed off from one railroad to the next on long train trips.

United and its predecessor airlines served U.S. cities and Vancouver, Canada, exclusively, but Pacific operations during World War II gave United experience flying beyond U.S. borders. In 1943, the Mexican government invited Patterson to Mexico City to evaluate the prospects of Líneas Aéreas Mineras, S.A. (LAMSA). The struggling carrier's purpose was to transport valuable minerals from mines deep within Mexico to U.S. markets and return with supplies and tools. The 1,700-mile route stretched from Mexico City to Juárez, just opposite El Paso, Texas, via Torreón.

Legendary United captain Jack Knight sums up the Age of Flight by spanning a globe with his fingers for (left to right) *United President Pat Patterson, first stewardess Ellen Church, and veteran captain E. Hamilton "Ham" Lee.*

By 1927, United was spreading its wings on the routes (right) *of four predecessor airlines (Boeing Air Transport, red; National Air Transport, green; Varney Air Lines, blue; and Pacific Air Transport, purple). It was "The Main Line Airway" by 1946. Hawai'i was added in 1947, and by 1970 United covered the United States. Colonel Roscoe Turner, on pages 182 and 183, flew his stock United Air Lines Boeing 247 to a second-place finish in the 11,323-mile London-to-Melbourne air race of 1935. The plane hangs in the main gallery of the Smithsonian Institution's National Air and Space Museum in Washington, DC.*

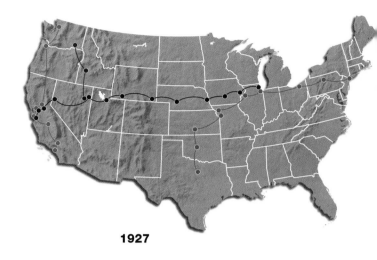

1927

Thwarted from expanding domestically, Patterson loaned LAMSA $250,000. Then he bought controlling interest in the Mexican carrier, making it a United subsidiary and renaming it Líneas Aéreas Mexicanas, S.A. Ultimately, United invested $5.6 million in LAMSA, and Patterson even sent United executives south to help run the operation. United planned to link its West Coast cities with LAMSA at Nogales. But United failed to win authority to serve Nogales, and the two carriers never established a common destination where they could transfer passengers.

After nine frustrating and expensive years, Patterson finally sold United's interest in LAMSA to local businessmen in 1952. The south-of-the-border lesson soured Patterson on expansion beyond U.S. borders. The corporate stance against operating internationally was destined to continue.

Patterson was so wary of international flying that, in mid-1943, United endorsed a proposal to designate Pan American as the country's sole flag carrier. Under that arrangement, United and other domestic lines would provide Pan Am with international passengers and receive a percentage of the profit. The proposal to make Pan Am the United States' chosen instrument never took hold. Having tasted the fruits of transoceanic operations during the war, many domestic carriers were eager to embrace the romance and renown of international routes. Not United. Patterson felt that passenger volume could not support all the eager new entries that would have to compete with the government-subsidized carriers of other nations, and chose instead to cultivate domestic routes—which in 1947 included the notable addition of Honolulu, his birthplace. United snapped up another line addition in 1947 when cash-short Western agreed to sell its Denver–Los Angeles route, a prize long coveted by Patterson.

After World War II, the Civil Aeronautics Board took steps to encourage experimental short-haul airlines to extend aviation's reach into smaller cities and towns. These smaller carriers served as feeder services bringing passengers to the major "trunkline" airways like United. Regional air-traffic growth was dramatic, and in 1955, 13 airlines were certified to operate as scheduled carriers. United's *Mainliner* magazine publicized these efforts and popularized the carriers with articles and advertisements recommending their services. Among the targeted beneficiaries were airlines such as Allegheny, Lake Central, Mohawk (which became USAir), and Piedmont (acquired by USAir before it became USAirways).

Although the Main Line stretched across the continent, United's routes had always been concentrated in the West. That changed dramatically in 1961. With the government's grudging consent, United acquired Capital Airlines, an aggressive but

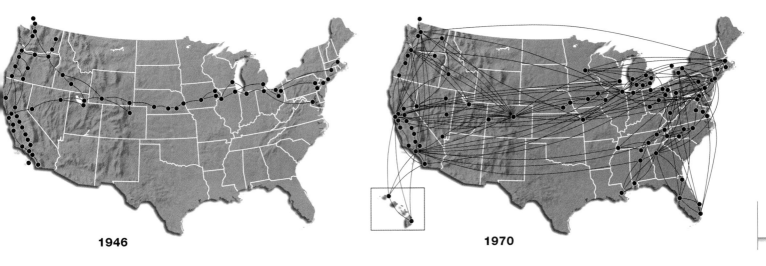

1946   **1970**

nearly bankrupt airline headquartered in Washington, DC. United's network suddenly included extensive routes throughout the East, stretching from Florida to the Great Lakes.

Despite some short-lived routes to Mexico and Canada in the 1930s, it was not until after Patterson retired that United really began venturing outside the United States. Even so, these routes remained modest by any standard. In addition to Vancouver, British Columbia, which United has served since 1934, United began service between Chicago and Toronto, Ontario, in 1967. Plans to become a bigger international player were set back severely in 1969 when the CAB denied every one of United's applications to serve destinations in the Far East while at the same time opening Hawai'i to service from other carriers.

In one of the most significant events in U.S. aviation history, the Airline Deregulation Act was passed in 1978, ending federal control of airline routes and fares. Carriers were free to select routes as they saw fit and to compete for passengers and freight in an open market. Though that freedom did not extend to international routes, United was more convinced than ever that its strong domestic network formed a solid foundation for international expansion.

In 1983 United finally received transpacific authority to serve Tokyo from Seattle. A trickle of service became a flood when United purchased Pan American's fabled Pacific Division in 1985 for $718 million and began flying to 13 Pacific cities in 1986.

Once established as a major carrier in the Pacific, United turned east and, in 1990, became a formidable transatlantic presence, as well. First it won government approval to serve Frankfurt and Paris from Chicago and Washington, DC. Then it made a key move into Europe by buying Pan Am's routes to London. Finally it closed the year by winning authority to serve Madrid from Washington, DC. Within the year United jetliners were flying to Berlin, Munich, and Amsterdam, and after Pan Am's demise, United acquired the carrier's Latin American routes, adding Caracas, Buenos Aires, Montevideo, Rio de Janeiro, São Paolo, and Santiago, among other South American cities in 1992.

Suddenly, the stylized *U* logo so familiar to the people in Hartford, Albuquerque, and Seattle was becoming a common sight in Hong Kong, Amsterdam, and Osaka. By the end of 1996, United was serving 39 destinations in 29 countries and two U.S. territories. International sales accounted for more than a third of the airline's total revenue.

United's popularity and established reputation in the United States and its focus on the Main Line while other carriers were being granted international routes had indeed provided the strong domestic platform it needed to become a significant

United grew quickly in the '90s. Its globe-girdling routes and partnerships now take customers almost anywhere. From small, primitive airfields along the United States' Main Line, United's destinations today include the great airports of the world.

international presence. But that was just the beginning.

United continued to pioneer partnerships with other airlines on international routes, despite the opposition of domestic competitors. Forging operating and marketing agreements in the 1990s with other premier carriers, including Air Canada, Lufthansa German Airlines, and Scandinavian Airline System (SAS), among others, United and these partner airlines offered one-stop check-in and coordinated their schedules to minimize waiting time for passengers switching from one carrier to the other. In many instances the two carriers involved would code share on flights. A single flight might have different flight numbers for each airline, but the airplane would be operated by the airline over whose route it was being flown.

The convenience of these code-sharing arrangements made them so popular with United's international passengers that in 1997 the airline moved to consolidate its global reach by joining with partners Air Canada, Lufthansa, SAS, and Thai International to form the Star Alliance. This huge code-share partnership served 578 cities in 106 countries by 2001.

The goal of the Alliance was to provide each airline's passengers with consistently superb, convenient, and hassle-free travel regardless of where they checked baggage, where they were going, or which carriers were involved with the itinerary. Accordingly, the member lines further coordinated schedules to facilitate transfers. Where possible, they co-located operations. For example, Lufthansa used United's gates in terminal 1 at Chicago O'Hare, and United used Lufthansa's gates in Frankfurt and Munich. And when passengers arrived at the ticket counter, they received boarding passes for all flights on all carriers involved, and baggage was checked through to the final destination.

Meanwhile, the mileage earned on a Star Alliance trip could be redeemed for reward travel on any Alliance airline. For example, miles accumulated on a domestic United flight or a transatlantic Lufthansa route could be redeemed to fly Thai International to Chiang Mai.

The benefits quickly grew. Qualified passengers were given access to more than 500 airport lounges throughout the world, and special dietary requests placed with one airline were passed along automatically to other carriers. To avoid having to send the inquiring passenger to the other airline's counter, agents at any member airline could access current information on the status of any other member airline's flights so they could advise about delays or gate changes instantly.

A good idea is hard to contain, and other carriers formed international groups as well. But the Star Alliance shone brightest, and not surprisingly, its constellation expanded. Within three years of its founding, the Alliance had grown to include Air New Zealand, Japan's All Nippon Airways, Ansett Australia, The Austrian Airlines Group, British Midland, Mexicana, Singapore Airlines, and Brazil's Varig—15 members in all, serving 130 countries on five continents. Combined, the group's 2,100 aircraft operate almost 10,000 flights daily to more than 800 destinations, more than three times the fleet, flights, and destinations served by United alone.

The Star Alliance, "The airline network for Earth," has become the largest airline partnership on the planet, a place that has shrunk considerably since homebody United decided the time had come to stretch its wings. The Main Line, the route of the pioneers, now reaches across the world. ⫿

Tokyo

Sydney

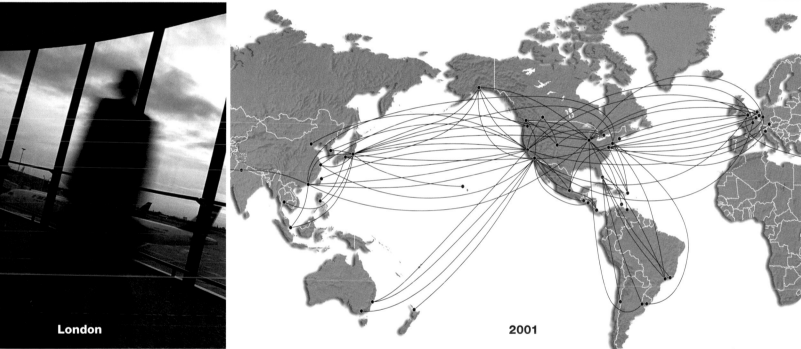

London

2001

Beijing

Frankfurt

A United 747 ferried 101st Airborne Division soldiers home from the Gulf War in 1991, part of a long tradition in the defense of freedom.

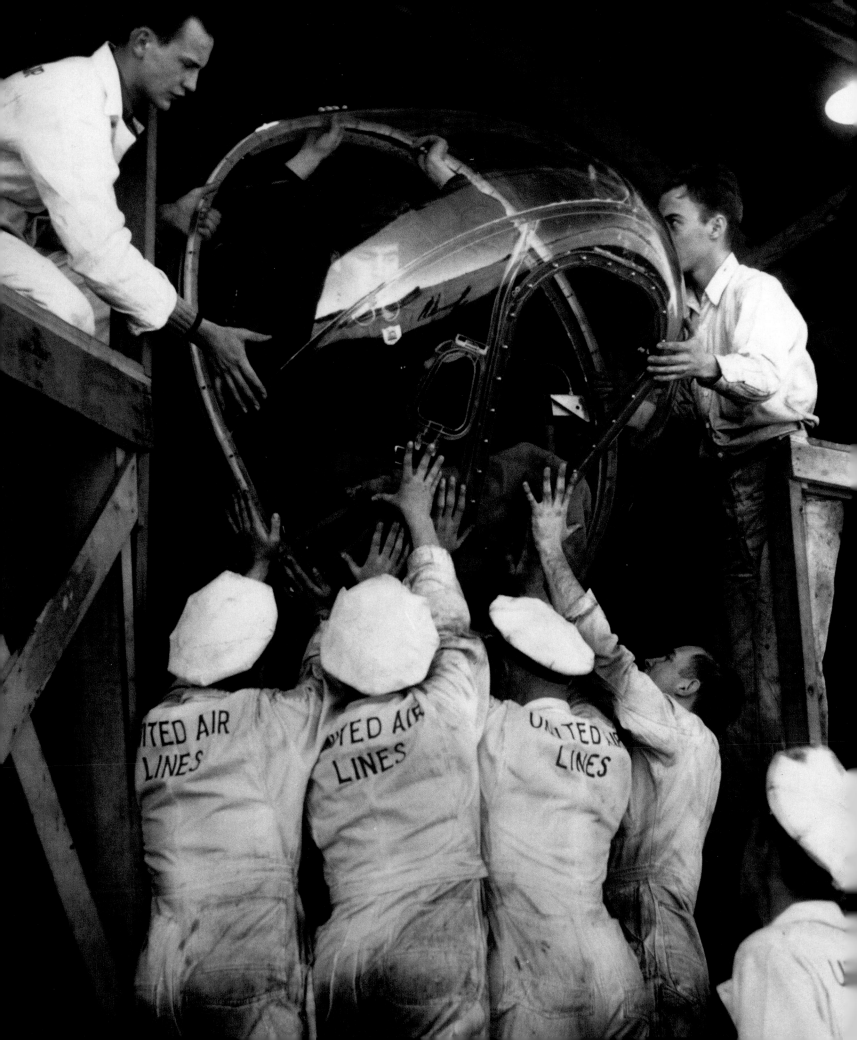

Civil aviation is clearly recognized as the backbone of defense. The country's welfare in time of peace and its safety in time of war rests on an economically sound air transportation system. —President Franklin Delano Roosevelt, 1939

UNITED GOES TO WAR | 193

By the time the United States entered World War II, aviation had developed into an elaborate transportation system with United and other U.S. airlines at the global cutting edge. The government looked to the airlines to help overcome military unpreparedness, and they swiftly stepped forward to serve—none more effectively than United.

Throughout the war, United operated air transport services, built and operated a huge aircraft modification center, and trained ground crews and pilots. The airline's Communications Center and flying laboratory were turned over to the military for vital research projects.

United personnel went to war in large numbers, flying bombers and fighters over Europe, and crawling through steaming island jungles. Thirty-six United employees died fighting for their country.

In the spring of 1942, only months after the United States entered the war, United turned over half of its fleet of airplanes and ground equipment to the government. The Air Transport Command then enlisted United to operate much of that equipment for the military. These planes were used to transport soldiers and deliver vital equipment around the world. In May 1942, United planes and pilots began an air link between the United States and American troops in Alaska, a link that proved vital when Japanese forces invaded Alaska's Aleutian Islands, the closest enemy ground forces got to the continental United States during the war. By September, United crews had begun flying supplies and personnel across the Pacific from San Francisco to Australia.

United's advertising stressed the role commercial airlines were playing in supporting the military. In one ad a plane recounted

They weren't pitching in to raise a battlefield flag, but United employees supported the cause, completing the assembly of more than 5,000 B-17 bombers (left). Pilots flying supplies wore the wings of the Air Transport Command (above).

its travels: On "an ordinary day like today, I covered 1,800 miles between 32 pairs of cities." The plane "rushed" government officials, military officers, and businessmen to their destinations, and "even found space for a famous actress touring the camps to give the boys a laugh ... As I go about my day's affairs, I wonder what America would have done for air transport in this highspeed war if the Airlines hadn't years ago laid the groundwork for it!"

"Cargoliners" were created by removing all the seats and installing special plywood flooring and steel-screened windows. These converted DC-3s were military workhorses, carrying just about any materiel imaginable—from plasma to parachutes to plane parts. United transported diesel engines to Wake Island, aluminum to Los Angeles, bomber parts to Dayton, and 10,000 pounds of

*United's wartime service to the nation was far-ranging and effective.
But it wasn't just United's pilots who flew into harm's way. United's stewardesses also went
to war. One of them became the most decorated woman in U.S. military history.*

FLIGHT NURSE DIARY / The year was 1938. And when Lillian Kinkella's mother suggested she might like being a "stewardess," the young nurse didn't know what the word meant. In fact, she'd never seen an airplane. But when she saw the glistening planes gathered at the United Air Lines Oakland, California, base, she was hooked. Within weeks, Kinkella was tending to passengers with the same care she'd given her patients.

Her flying life started in Boeing 247s. She still thrills to the fact that her first flight aboard a DC-3 was captained by "Ham" Lee, a legendary United airman who had once flown airmail in an open-cockpit biplane. She met Eleanor Roosevelt—who knitted during a weather delay—and she had a date with Cary Grant.

After the United States entered World War II, Kinkella was confronted one day by a passenger. "What are you doing on this plane?" he asked. "You're a registered nurse and we have a war going on." Why, he wondered, wasn't she serving as a flight nurse. She'd never heard of that job but soon discovered that nurses were aboard the military aircraft evacuating wounded servicemen from combat areas. Several United stewardesses—then all registered nurses—had already become flight nurses. Within weeks, she joined them.

She crossed the Atlantic on a troop ship and by the summer of 1943, she was in England pulling wounded and frostbitten crewmen out of B-17s just returned from bombing raids. It was a time she'll never forget; the terrible wounds, the grateful young men. She witnessed the first buzz bomb attack on London, and in June 1944, she climbed aboard a C-47 heading for France. D-Day had come, and she was going to collect the fallen.

It was incredibly dangerous work. "Our plane wasn't permitted to have a Red Cross on the side," she says matter-of-factly. "It was always sent off full of supplies"—highly explosive munitions.

Moments after the aircraft touched down, soldiers pulled out the cargo while Kinkella lowered the straps to support the litters. And then they arrived. Men—boys, mostly—shot in the head, the chest, the legs. En route to England, Kinkella moved from one man to the next, stanching the flow of blood, giving medicine and comfort. After the patients were delivered, the C-47 headed back to the front. She made 250 evacuation flights—23 of them transatlantic. Kinkella returned to United as an assistant chief stewardess. One postwar highlight came in 1947 when her DC-6 took off from Honolulu on the airline's first flight from Hawai'i to the Mainland.

Her return was short-lived. With the outbreak of war in Korea, U.S. Air Force Captain Kinkella headed to the front again. Over the next 16 months, she flew 175 air evacuations. Back home, she served the Air Force as a nurse and public speaker, and worked as a technical adviser on the 1953 movie inspired by her life—*Flight Nurse*.

In 1954 Kinkella married former Navy officer Walter Keil. She left the service and United to devote herself to her family. In 1961, her appearance on the popular TV series *This Is Your Life* garnered one of the 10 highest mail responses in the show's history. Many of the letters were from the wounded veterans she had helped.

Her children are grown now, and Walter passed away in 1980, but Lillian Kinkella Keil retains the same positive spirit that took her into the air so many years ago. Looking back at her time serving United customers and her country, she says, "I've certainly had a wonderful career. I'd do it all over again."

For her selflessness, Lillian Kinkella Keil was awarded 19 medals, including a European Theater medal with four battle stars, a Korean service medal with seven battle stars, and four Air Medals. She is believed to be the most decorated woman in U.S. military history. ///

The wartime service of former United stewardess Lillian Kinkella Keil (far right) was dramatized in the 1953 movie Flight Nurse. Actress Joan Leslie (near right) played Keil. Forrest Tucker costarred.

By World War II's end, the Pacific Ocean had become familiar territory for United crews. Back in the States, company posters constantly reminded United employees of the role they played in winning the fight (right)*. This one resembled a military recruitment poster.*

machine guns and ammunition to Alaska. United crews flew to Hawai'i, Australia, Guam, Guadalcanal, the Fiji Islands, and, finally, Tokyo. In four years, United crews flew 50 million miles, ferrying 156,000 military passengers and 8,600 tons of cargo on more than 7,000 crossings of the Pacific Ocean.

To fulfill the desperate need for bombers in all combat theaters at the beginning of the war, United transformed its massive maintenance facility in Cheyenne, Wyoming, into a bomber modification center. There United workers on post-manufacture production lines made last-minute alterations such as installing machine-gun mounts, rebuilding tail turret assemblies, and installing microphone switches on gun grips before sending the B-17s overseas. Eventually 1,600 men and "Rosie the Riveters" were employed at the center, many of them living in temporary trailers or newly built dormitories. Two 64,000-square-foot hangars were built to shelter the scores of bombers being worked on. By the conclusion of the war, the Cheyenne operation had manufactured over 4 million aircraft parts and had prepared 5,736 Flying Fortresses (B-17s) for combat.

During the war, commercial instruction ceased at United's Boeing School of Aeronautics in Oakland, California, and all efforts turned to training 5,000 technicians and mechanics for the Army and Navy. In addition, specialized on-the-job training was given to line mechanics and radio mechanics at maintenance centers throughout the United system. Pilots for the Air Transport Command were trained at the Denver center.

Several thousand United employees were drafted or volunteered for service. The company put them on military leave of absence and they continued gaining seniority while in the service, as well as receiving an annual Christmas bonus. These men and women served in a variety of positions, including combat pilots, flight nurses, and line mechanics, in just about every theater of the war.

United's Clayton Joyce was chief pilot of the India-China wing of the Air Transport Command, responsible for the famous airlift over "The Hump," the Himalaya Mountains.

When the Air Corps asked United to supply crews to fly VIPs on important missions, one of the pilots selected was veteran Weldon "Dusty" Rhoades. The assignment involved carrying military and State Department personnel to Cairo for a meeting of President Roosevelt, Winston Churchill, and Chiang Kai-shek. Among the passengers on the 31,380-mile flight was General Douglas MacArthur's chief of staff, who recommended Rhoades to his boss. Soon the United airman was in an Army Air Corps uniform and piloting MacArthur's plane, *The Bataan*. And in August 1945, Rhoades landed *The Bataan* in Tokyo where MacArthur accepted the Japanese surrender. Twelve other planes operated by United crews flew into the Japanese capital for the long-awaited event that ended the most terrible conflict in history.

At the conclusion of the war, United Airlines received numerous awards and honors for its contributions. Incredibly, even while on a wartime schedule, the airline had more than doubled in size.

During World War II, the government paid United for its work, but months after the fighting ended, government auditors arrived to reconcile the books. Pat Patterson was ready for them. "We've audited the books," he explained, "and we think we

should reimburse the government $296,000." With that, he proudly wrote out a check for the full amount.

United's role in World War II also involved an experimental four-engine successor to the DC-3. Prior to the war, United pledged to pay for a large share of the development of the aircraft and Douglas did build a triple-tail transport called the DC-4E. But United wasn't impressed. Though that design was never produced, it led to the successful C-54 Skymaster military transport and the postwar DC-4.

United's return to mufti was short-lived. Less than two weeks after fighting began in Korea in 1950, the airline was once again airlifting personnel and equipment across the Pacific, this time to staging airports in Japan. Meanwhile, many employees exchanged United uniforms for government issue and went back into the fray. Over the next three years, United planes and crews flew more than 1,000 roundtrips between San Francisco and Tokyo, carrying 25,000 troops, 3,000 tons of mail, 355 tons of blood and medical supplies, and 260 tons of ammunition.

When hostilities erupted in Southeast Asia in the 1960s, United responded as before, with a transpacific airlift of troops and war supplies along the Bamboo Route between California and Vietnam and Thailand in DC-8 jetliners and freighters. More than 600 employees took leave of their jobs to lead ground patrols, join helicopter crews, and fly from carriers cruising in the South China Sea.

United, along with 30 other airlines, participates in the Civil Reserve Air Fleet (CRAF), an agreement under which commercial aircraft can be called upon by the Pentagon in times of national emergency to provide immediate additional airlift. Another call came in 1990 after Iraqi troops poured across the border into Kuwait. The U.S. responded by sending half a million troops to the Persian Gulf—including more than 300 United employees—many of them aboard five United 747s assigned to CRAF missions. All totaled, United aircraft and crews flew more than 200 CRAF flights from the United States and European air bases to the Persian Gulf carrying troops and cargo in support of Operation Desert Storm.

When called upon, United has always been ready to lend its expertise and muscle to the protection of the United States and its allies. But the planes it flies and those who fly them make their most valuable contribution when bringing people together in peace. ///

1929   1937   1938   1954   1955

1926 — **Walter T. Varney's airline**, one of **United's** four founding carriers, launches the first sustained commercial airmail service.

1927 — **National Air Transport** and **Boeing Air Transport**, two of **United's** founding carriers, offer the United States' first scheduled coast-to-coast passenger service. And with American Railway Express Company, **BAT** and **NAT** offer the first coast-to-coast air express service for cargo.

1929 — **Boeing Air Transport** offers the first complete courses in aviation occupations through its Boeing School of Aeronautics.

BAT develops a practical system of two-way, plane-to-ground voice radio communication later adopted by the entire airline industry.

1930 — **Boeing Air Transport** employs eight young nurses as "stewardesses" on its Model 80A, thus creating a new and liberating career for women that all other carriers would eventually copy.

1933 — **United's** constituent carriers are the first to begin service with the Boeing 247, the first modern airliner.

1936 — **United** is the first airline to open a kitchen designed solely for the preparation of food to be served to passengers in flight.

1937 — **United** is first to establish a "flying laboratory," a Boeing 247-D that tests wing deicing systems, fuel injection carburetors, and other groundbreaking equipment.

1938 — **United** is the first airline to standardize the use of controllable pitch and constant speed propellers and to install full-feathering props.

United is the first transportation company to install two-way, coast-to-coast teletype service.

1939 — **United** develops the static discharger, a device on the trailing edges of wings and elevators that discharges static electricity to prevent interference with aircraft radio reception. The device is subsequently adopted by the entire airline industry.

1948 — **United** develops and is first to use the instrument landing system (ILS).

1950 — **United** is the first airline to provide a special container permitting the shipment of dogs on the same flight as their owners.

1951 — **United** operates the United States' first VHF (Very High Frequency) radio network.

1954 — **United** is the first domestic airline to use electronic flight simulators for advanced training of flight crews.

United begins testing the Air Dock, precursor of today's telescoping passenger loading bridge.

1955 — **United** is the first airline to use and make C-Band weather radar standard equipment.

United is the first domestic airline to order jetliners—30 Douglas DC-8s.

United is the first airline to use closed circuit television to display flight information in airports.

1956 — **United** is the first airline to install and use an automatic conveyor system for baggage handling at major terminals.

1955

1956

1982

1995

2002

1959 — **United** is the first airline to use computers for flight plan forecasting. The computers select the best combination of "tracks" for long-range jet flights in terms of weather, altitude, flying time, and fuel burn.

1960 — **United** is the first airline to begin service with the Boeing 720 four-engine jetliner.

1961 — **United** installs the Instamatic electronic reservations system—largest interconnected electronic data-processing facility ever built for business use.

1964 — **United** is the first airline to begin operational testing of automatic altitude reporting, in cooperation with the Federal Aviation Administration.

United is the first U.S. airline to install and test a fully automatic, all-weather landing system.

1965 — **United** is the first airline to qualify for FAA Category II, all-weather program, allowing DC-8s to land at specific airports with ceilings as low as 150 feet and visibility of only ⅜ mile.

1968 — **United** is the first U.S. airline to begin service with the Boeing 737.

1974 — **United** is the first airline to offer automated ticketing, providing faster ticket service for travel agencies and commercial accounts.

1982 — **United** is the first airline to begin service with the Boeing 767 twin-engine widebody jet.

1984 — **United** is the first airline to train pilots to respond to the dangers of wind shear by providing realistic scenarios in flight simulators.

1988 — **United** pioneers the use of the first airborne Traffic Collision Avoidance System (TCAS).

1990 — **United** is the first airline to implement the satellite-based data communications (SATCOM) system on a commercial jetliner. The service allows clear, quick, and uninterrupted communications between the cockpit and ground controllers.

1995 — **United** is the first airline to fly the Boeing 777, the world's largest twin-engine jumbo jet. The design was heavily influenced by United.

United is the first airline to operate the Future Air Navigation System (FANS) using the satellite-based Global Positioning System (GPS).

1996 — **United** is the first airline to receive FAA approval for use of the Enhanced Ground Proximity Warning System (EGPWS), providing pilots more time to avoid threatening terrain.

1998 — **United** is the first commercial airline with fleetwide air recirculation filters that meet the true High Efficiency Particulate Air (HEPA) standard.

2002 — **United** crews and a United 747SP are chosen for SOFIA, the Stratospheric Observatory for Infrared Astronomy.

WHAT
MAN CAN
IMAGINE,
HE CAN DO...

For I dipt into the future
Far as human eye could se
Vision of the worl
e wonder that w
e heavens fill with
es of magic sails
purple tw

NC-417H

Adrian Delfino was United's historian during a more than 30-year career. Here he remembers three decades of encounters with the airline's pioneers.

REMEMBRANCE OF TIMES PAST |

WHEN I OFFICIALLY RETIRED IN 1987, AFTER LABORING FOR 32 YEARS IN UNITED'S CORPORATE COMMUNICATIONS vineyard, almost half of those years as company historian where I authored the second volume of United's corporate and legal history, I had no way of knowing that I'd just be entering another phase in a long association with the company I love. I continue to serve United, currently as the ex officio historian and archival consultant.

I believe that once you pass a certain number of years of service, United becomes a permanent part of your life. Check the many active retiree groups all over the country and click on the various Web sites spawned by "homesick" United alumni.

United has been a big part of my family. My son and a daughter, both working toward retirement at United, have racked up a combined seniority of more than 50 years. I also have a couple of nephews and an ex-daughter-in-law who are still working for the company and have logged close to three-quarters of a century. Just recently, one of my nephews retired after 34 years with United. There are many such connections in the United family.

I have often been asked, "What has it been like to work for United?" I am sure that question is asked of hundreds of retired pilots, flight attendants, mechanics, and station and office personnel. And they most likely respond with tales of exciting moments, camaraderie, and a passion for their jobs. In many ways, that's still how it is at United. The cast has certainly increased vastly and our stage is now truly the world. But the courage and commitment of the early United pioneers can still be found in the company.

Former United historian Adrian Delfino in 1965 with Pat Patterson (left). **Delfino's years with company executives convinced him that "What man can imagine, he can do" is an apt expression of the United spirit.**

I am now one of the last links between the United Airlines of open-cockpit airplanes and the global air transport giant of today. And I have accumulated a mental and emotional warehouse of precious memories, many of them from tales told to me by the courageous pioneers who built United.

As company historian, I made friends with Harlan "Bud" Gurney, who was Charles Lindbergh's barnstorming partner before Lindy's legendary transatlantic flight from New York to Paris in 1927. I interviewed Leon Cuddeback, who launched Walter Varney's epochal flight on April 6, 1926, and paved the way for United Airlines. I visited with Steve Stimpson, the flamboyant Boeing Air Transport sales executive who gave the world its first airline stewardess. I listened to stories spun by

The first of United's 40 Convair 340 Mainliners is christened in 1952. The watching stewardesses wore a variety of vintage uniforms.

Adrian Delfino has helped record United's history. He helped write Airway One *(1974) with United's R.E. Johnson. He also provided final review for the airline's other historical volumes;* High Horizons *(1964),* Of Magic Sails *(1975), and* Pat Patterson *(1967).*

Russ Cunningham and Bill Lawrenz, who helped the eccentric genius Thorp Hiscock during the developmental phase of ground-to-air radio. And I picked up mementos from Hamilton "Ham" Lee, the world's "flyingest man" during his time, who precipitated the first pilot strike against the United States Air Mail Service.

I'll never forget them, including the United interviewer in San Francisco who, on September 23, 1954, read my application for a ramp service position, took one look at my 98-pound body and said, "Look, kid ... those bags weigh twice as much as you." Instead, he gave me the job of general clerk, and I kept track of the airline's daily gas and oil inventories at United's maintenance base in the city.

Although officially classified as a clerk, I became an unofficial member of the corporate PR staff when they heard of my journalistic training and previous work as reporter and night editor for a Chicago newspaper. They soon had me working with company photographers on articles for the employee publication.

There are so many people who are etched in my mind. Charles F. McErlean, who retired as assistant chairman of the board at United, offered me the first and only corporate historian position at United when he was the airline's general counsel and senior vice president of law.

Nor can I forget Jack Tordoff, one of the true renaissance men who worked for United. A professional jeweler before he joined the airline, Jack was a talented musician and was well-read in the arts, history, science, and technology. He made and repaired violins and was a skillful violinist. Above all, he was a keen observer of human nature, and it was on him that I leaned for answers to questions about the quality of the men who led United through the years. A co-organizer of the mechanics union, he later served as company representative on contract negotiations. Not once did he turn his back on United, nor did he ever betray former colleagues in the machinists' ranks. If any man could play fair, it was Jack.

I knew Charlie Wrightson, Varney's traffic manager at Boise, Idaho, who helped unload the first sacks of mail Leon Cuddeback flew in from Pasco, Washington, on that historic day of April 6, 1926. Charlie gave me a precious gift for United's museum collection—a Remington rifle issued to Varney's pilots to protect the U.S. mail but used more frequently to shoot rabbits when pilots were forced down and needed something to eat.

And there was Curtis Barkes, who joined National Air Transport as an office boy in 1925. A scholarly looking executive with gentle eyes, a soft voice, and a shy smile, Curtis masterminded the 1961 merger that brought Capital Airlines into the United fold and ended, at least until 2001, the seesaw battle between United and American Airlines for title of the world's largest commercial carrier.

And who among United's old-timers can forget Pat Patterson? It was he who launched United's history program, which gave birth to seven historical volumes and two minimuseums in lobbies at the airline's executive offices.

Born on a sugar plantation on the island of Oʻahu in Hawaiʻi, Patterson went to live with his grandfather in Honolulu after his father died of malaria. His widowed mother had to leave him so that she could pursue office skills on the mainland that would bring her a better life. The young boy soon sailed with his grandmother on the schooner *Annie Johnson* to join his mother on the mainland, where his incredible transitions from grammar school boy to bank office boy and junior officer to airline executive and industry leader would all transpire.

Unlike many political or business leaders, the affable Patterson was never an enigma to those around him. Gifted with a keen perception of people and events, he could anticipate with uncanny ability the responses he would get from associates during a meeting. On the other hand, his gregarious nature and up-front style of dealing with people made it easy for others to read him. Patterson's reign at United brought him many friends and admirers. And his admirers included not only United employees but also their spouses. For every child born to a United employee or spouse, Patterson made sure that a blue or pink blanket was sent to the child.

Someone once asked me, "What kind of a leader was Patterson? Was he stern and autocratic?" Stern? Yes, but not in a harsh or severe way. And he was autocratic, but more in a "let's-try-doing-it-my-way" sense of the word. On at least three occasions, he realized doing it "his way" did not work. His experiment in One-Class Service, his adamant refusal to serve liquor aloft, and his firm stand on keeping United a domestic carrier were all reversed in his lifetime.

When Patterson retired in 1966, among the souvenirs unveiled for his farewell was a scale model of the schooner on which he had crossed the Pacific to San Francisco. Patterson stood dumbfounded for what seemed like an eternity. And then he slowly muttered, "I'll be damned. It's the *Annie Johnson.*"

More than a generation has passed since the Patterson era came to a close. Each man who followed him in the executive suite has left his own mark. George Keck made the first attempt to globalize United and gave the company record-setting revenue gains. He commented to me one day, when snow lay piled at the base of a willow tree in one of the courtyards at World Headquarters, "Look at all that snow. In times like this, don't you wish we were back in San Francisco?" In retrospect, I think he never felt as at home as he did back in the Bay Area.

Eddie Carlson, who replaced George Keck as CEO, was a totally different creature. Like Patterson, he was a short man who was bigger than life. And like Patterson, he tried to bring the rank and file into his world. In his first few weeks at United, Eddie made a whirlwind tour of the system to hear what the airline's employees wanted to say. After he returned, he stopped me one day to say he had met my son, a daughter, and three nephews—all named Delfino—when he stopped at San Francisco.

"What the hell are you trying to do," he said, "take over the airline?" Several days later, we met again and he sidled up to me and ran one hand across the top of our heads. "Adrian," he said to me, "it's little guys like us who will turn this airline around." He sure knew how to make short guys feel 6 feet tall.

These are only a few of the vignettes I savored during my years at United. They're still happening to United's men and women today. And they'll continue to happen because we're all actors in this far-flung, never-ending play. Today's employees may speak different tongues, but they continue to share a unified goal—moving the company into the future while taking customers all over the world.

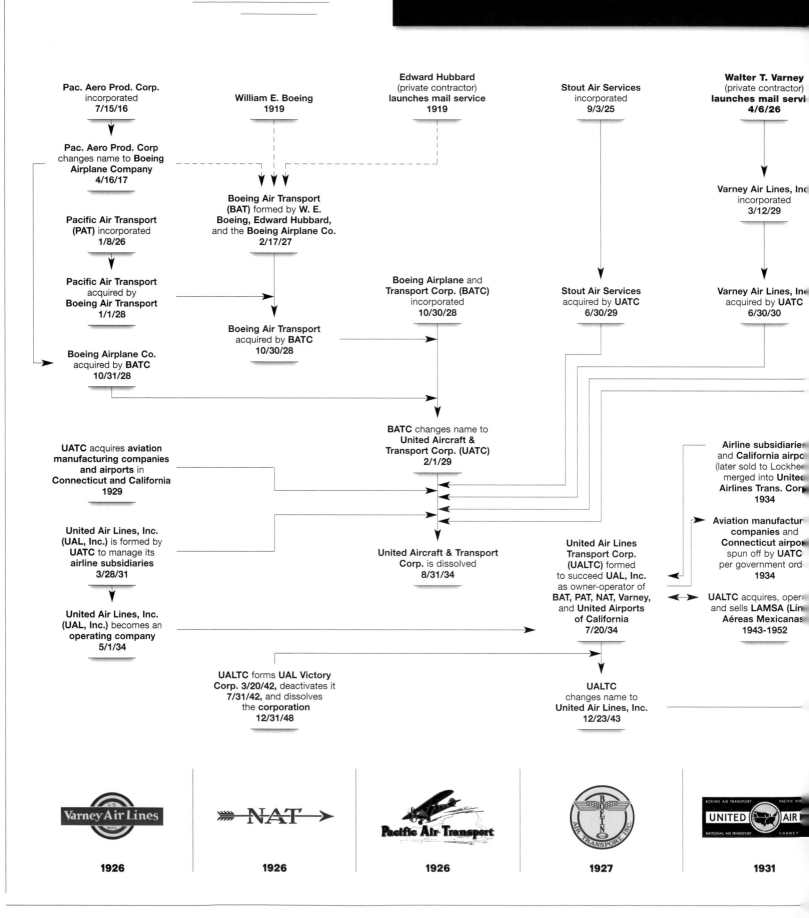

Pac. Aero Prod. Corp.
incorporated
7/15/16

↓

Pac. Aero Prod. Corp
changes name to **Boeing Airplane Company**
4/16/17

Pacific Air Transport (PAT) incorporated
1/8/26

↓

Pacific Air Transport acquired by **Boeing Air Transport**
1/1/28

Boeing Airplane Co. acquired by **BATC**
10/31/28

William E. Boeing
1919

Boeing Air Transport (BAT) formed by **W. E. Boeing, Edward Hubbard,** and the **Boeing Airplane Co.**
2/17/27

Boeing Air Transport acquired by **BATC**
10/30/28

Edward Hubbard
(private contractor)
launches mail service
1919

Boeing Airplane and **Transport Corp. (BATC)** incorporated
10/30/28

Stout Air Services
incorporated
9/3/25

Stout Air Services acquired by **UATC**
6/30/29

Walter T. Varney
(private contractor)
launches mail servi
4/6/26

Varney Air Lines, Inc
incorporated
3/12/29

↓

Varney Air Lines, Inc acquired by **UATC**
6/30/30

BATC changes name to **United Aircraft & Transport Corp. (UATC)**
2/1/29

UATC acquires aviation manufacturing companies and airports in **Connecticut and California**
1929

United Air Lines, Inc. (UAL, Inc.) is formed by **UATC** to manage its **airline subsidiaries**
3/28/31

↓

United Air Lines, Inc. (UAL, Inc.) becomes an **operating company**
5/1/34

United Aircraft & Transport Corp. is dissolved
8/31/34

United Air Lines Transport Corp. (UALTC) formed to succeed **UAL, Inc.** as owner-operator of **BAT, PAT, NAT, Varney,** and **United Airports of California**
7/20/34

Airline subsidiaries and **California airpo** (later sold to Lockhee merged into **Unitec Airlines Trans. Cor** 1934

Aviation manufactur companies and **Connecticut airpo** spun off by **UATC** per government ord 1934

UALTC acquires, oper and sells **LAMSA (Lír Aéreas Mexicanas** 1943-1952

UALTC forms UAL Victory Corp. 3/20/42, deactivates it 7/31/42, and dissolves the **corporation**
12/31/48

UALTC changes name to **United Air Lines, Inc.**
12/23/43

1926

1926

1926

1927

1931

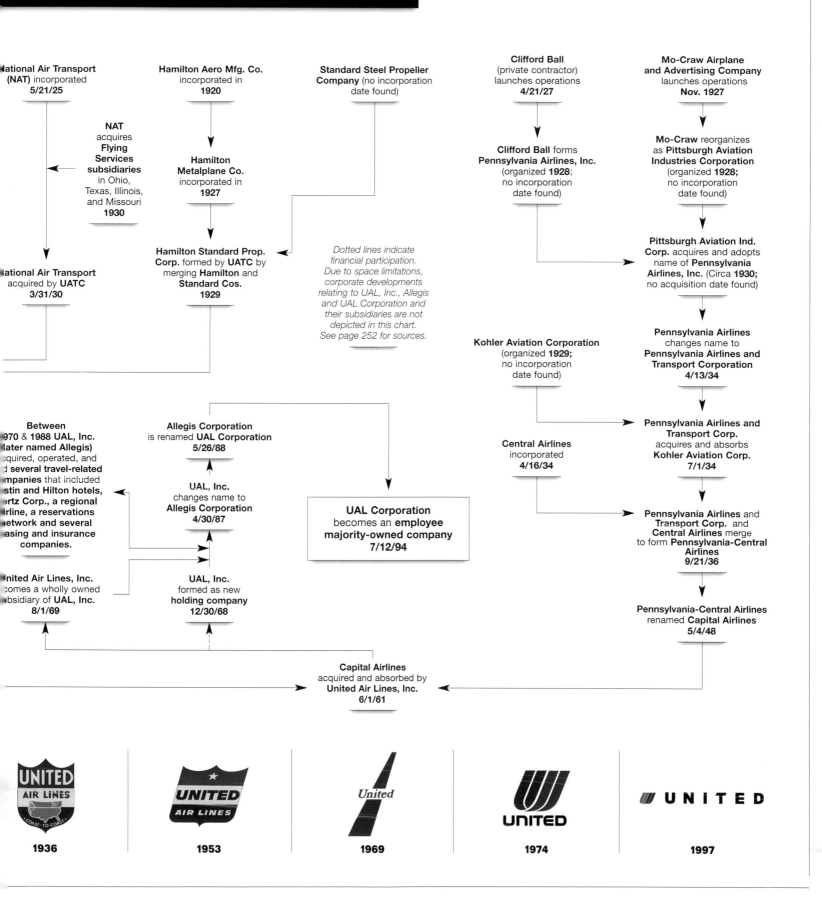

National Air Transport (NAT) incorporated 5/21/25

NAT acquires Flying Services subsidiaries in Ohio, Texas, Illinois, and Missouri 1930

National Air Transport acquired by UATC 3/31/30

Hamilton Aero Mfg. Co. incorporated in 1920

Hamilton Metalplane Co. incorporated in 1927

Hamilton Standard Prop. Corp. formed by UATC by merging **Hamilton** and **Standard** Cos. 1929

Standard Steel Propeller Company (no incorporation date found)

Dotted lines indicate financial participation. Due to space limitations, corporate developments relating to UAL, Inc., Allegis and UAL Corporation and their subsidiaries are not depicted in this chart. See page 252 for sources.

Clifford Ball (private contractor) launches operations 4/21/27

Clifford Ball forms Pennsylvania Airlines, Inc. (organized **1928**; no incorporation date found)

Kohler Aviation Corporation (organized **1929**; no incorporation date found)

Central Airlines incorporated 4/16/34

Mo-Craw Airplane and Advertising Company launches operations **Nov. 1927**

Mo-Craw reorganizes as Pittsburgh Aviation Industries Corporation (organized **1928**; no incorporation date found)

Pittsburgh Aviation Ind. Corp. acquires and adopts name of Pennsylvania Airlines, Inc. (Circa **1930**; no acquisition date found)

Pennsylvania Airlines changes name to Pennsylvania Airlines and Transport Corporation 4/13/34

Pennsylvania Airlines and Transport Corp. acquires and absorbs Kohler Aviation Corp. 7/1/34

Pennsylvania Airlines and Transport Corp. and Central Airlines merge to form Pennsylvania-Central Airlines 9/21/36

Pennsylvania-Central Airlines renamed Capital Airlines 5/4/48

Between 1970 & 1988 UAL, Inc. (later named Allegis) acquired, operated, and several travel-related companies that included ...stin and Hilton hotels, ...rtz Corp., a regional ...irline, a reservations ...etwork and several ...asing and insurance companies.

United Air Lines, Inc. ...comes a wholly owned ...bsidiary of **UAL, Inc.** 8/1/69

Allegis Corporation is renamed UAL Corporation 5/26/88

UAL, Inc. changes name to Allegis Corporation 4/30/87

UAL, Inc. formed as new holding company 12/30/68

UAL Corporation becomes an employee majority-owned company 7/12/94

Capital Airlines acquired and absorbed by United Air Lines, Inc. 6/1/61

UNITED AIR LINES COAST-TO-COAST 1936

UNITED AIR LINES 1953

United 1969

UNITED 1974

UNITED 1997

The balance sheet of United Airlines places no dollars and cents value on our employees but in my opinion they represent the most important asset our company has on the books. —W. A. PATTERSON

THE START OF THE 20TH CENTURY'S FINAL DECADE WAS A DIFFICULT PERIOD FOR UNITED. THE CRISIS FOLLOWING Iraq's invasion of Kuwait in 1990 sent the price of fuel—one of an airline's major expenses—soaring. The United States' economy was in recession and business travel was down. Meanwhile, deregulation of the air transport industry in the United States in 1978 had given rise to numerous low-cost carriers, many of whom were competing for United's customers.

It all made for grim accounting. The airline reported a record net 1991 loss of $332 million and a staggering 1992 loss of $957 million—more than $100,000 for every hour of every day in the year. In 1993 the loss was $50 million. Something had to be done.

The company responded by discontinuing unprofitable routes. It grounded dozens of older, high-maintenance aircraft and negotiated delays in the delivery schedule on scores of ordered airliners. Many employees took pay cuts or had raises deferred. It sought and won price concessions from hundreds of vendors, sold 16 of its 17 domestic flight kitchens, which employed more than 5,000, and began outsourcing janitorial, sky cap, and many other functions formerly performed by United employees. In addition, the company eliminated 1,900 unfilled positions and furloughed 2,800 employees. It was a very dark period.

As with many businesses, employee compensation and benefits represented a substantial portion of the company's costs. If a method could be found to meaningfully reduce that expense, the airline would be in a much stronger position. One such approach had been broached in April of 1987. Just weeks after United's parent company changed its name from UAL, Inc. to Allegis Corporation, a group led by the airline's pilots initiated moves to acquire ownership.

Buttons proclaimed the 1994 news that employees owned the company (left). The annual report (page 213) showed employee-owners at the N.Y. Stock Exchange. A 1990 button touts revenue passenger mile performance (above).

Reacting to Wall Street rumblings that Allegis' subsidiaries were worth more individually than the parent company's stock price indicated, the employee-led group, consisting of pilots, flight attendants, machinists, and both management and salaried employees, tried but couldn't amass financial backing for the takeover. Allegis, meanwhile, had sold off its non-airline subsidiaries, while changing its name to UAL Corporation and returning to its original core operation as an airline. In the complex and turbulent years that followed, the employees' effort resurfaced.

By mid-1993, the employee buyout project had moved closer to realization. On labor's side, wage cuts and work rule changes involving 54,000 employees were projected to save the airline nearly $5 billion over the first six years of the Employee Stock Ownership Plan. In response, employees

As this 2001 United Services ad aptly expresses, it's the pride and professionalism of United's people that brings the company into focus.

would see their equity grow to 55 percent over the same period. In addition, representatives for the participating employees—pilots, machinists, and salaried/management groups—would be elected to the board of directors.

The UAL Corporation board agreed to the proposal in December 1993, and stockholders approved it the following July. People who worked at United owned the company—the world's largest majority employee-owned corporation. Badges proclaimed, "We don't just work here" and "Proud Owner."

The benefits of this unprecedented arrangement were soon evident. The fiscal hemorrhaging had been reversed. The reborn United posted a profit of $51 million.

Pat Patterson had long ago realized that aggressively soliciting the opinions and participation of United employees was a key ingredient in the task of inventing a new industry. His United had created the industry's first credit union in 1935 and its first employee medical department in 1937. United's employee-focus was further built on collective bargaining agreements—with the Airmen's Association of America in 1939, the Air Line Pilots Association in 1940, the International Association of Machinists in 1945, and the Air Line Stewardesses Association in 1946. An employee retirement program debuted in 1941, and 1946 saw a 40-hour workweek. So it is fitting that United employees took the initiative to pioneer another new vision.

At the start of the new century, United is an organization imbued with ownership—employee ownership of the company itself, and ownership of one of the richest traditions in aviation. Leadership is the core of that tradition.

Ever since the days of the flying laboratory, United has been known for second-to-none standards of safety, maintenance, training, and technology. United has set industry standards by pioneering the newest technology—not just by adopting it.

In 1995, United set out to extend the world-class quality of its operational services to airlines around the world with the launch of United Services, one of a growing number of businesses within the business of United Airlines. United Services builds on the airline's early and ongoing leadership with flight simulators and unequalled maintenance expertise to create safer skies for pilots and passengers around the world. It even provides superb ground-handling operations for more than 200 carriers.

As in the past, when United's leading-edge capabilities reach outside the airline, it is aviation and the flying public who benefit.

Building on the mid-1990s invention of the electronic ticket, United's technological leadership enters a new century exploring "company-within-a-company" e-commerce initiatives to improve customer service, boost earnings, and cut costs with Internet and wireless-based technology. United launched the first real time availability of flight information on hand-held PDAs.

Self-service was the focus of 2001 initiatives like EasyCheck-in℠ units and EasyInfo℠ gate room information screens—part of the largest deployment of airport customer service innovations by any airline ever. Proactive re-booking of customers with disrupted travel plans was part of the effort.

United employees face a new century, a new economy, and the challenge of navigating the inevitable workplace issues encountered in any complex organization. But today's United is a collection of people who've stepped forward not just to lobby for their own interests within the organization, but to vest the company with their dreams and futures and to once again, create a new kind of airline.

With unmatched professionalism and an enduring sense of pride, United faces its second 75 years poised to do what it did in its first—invent the future of commercial aviation. ✈

1927 1930 1936 1938 1953

1927	**National Air Transport** and **Boeing Air Transport**, two of **United's** founding carriers, offer the United States' first scheduled coast-to-coast passenger service. **BAT** provides passengers with inflight meals.
1930	**Boeing Air Transport** hires the first stewardesses. The eight young women, all nurses, work aboard the line's Boeing 80A trimotors operating between San Francisco and Chicago.
1936	**United** opens the airline industry's first flight kitchen, gaining direct control over the quality of food service. The cuisine is crafted by European chefs.
1938	**United** is the first airline to permit guide dogs to ride with their blind owners in the passenger cabin.
1938	**United** begins a "take your wife free" campaign that is relaunched in the 1960s as "Take Me Along." Both permit wives to accompany fare-paying husbands for free.
1940	**United** is the first airline to offer low-cost air coach service—on 10-passenger Boeing 247Ds flying between San Francisco and Los Angeles—and the first airline to operate all cargo flights.
1946	**United** is the first airline to offer charters for professional football teams, transporting the Chicago Rockets, Los Angeles Dons, Miami Seahawks, Buffalo Bisons, and Cleveland Browns, among others.
1947	**United** is the first airline to install radio telephones for inflight use by passengers.
1950	**United** is the first airline to permit dogs to travel on the same flights as their owners. The service uses the Tuttle Kennel, a special sanitized container invented by United's medical director, Colonel A.D. Tuttle. It is replaced by the Mainliner Kennel in 1960.
1953	**United** inaugurates men-only "Executive Flights" featuring complimentary steaks and cigars. Program continues until 1970.
1954	**United** begins testing the Air Dock, an enclosed gangway that permits passengers to walk directly onto an aircraft without climbing stairs. From these early experiments emerged today's telescoping passenger loading bridges.
1954	**United** is the first airline to offer "self-claiming" baggage service. The system enables passengers to pick up their own luggage from open racks without waiting to present claim checks to attendants.
1957	**United** is the first airline to publish an inflight magazine for passengers.

1954   1954   1957   1966   2001

1960   **United** is the first airline to offer High-Speed Ticketing. Selected customers can write their own simplified tickets, reducing ticketing time by 75 percent.

1961   **United** introduces its Instamatic reservations system, the largest interconnected data-processing system ever built for private industry.

1966   **United** is the first airline to sell cocktails to passengers in Economy Class.

1967   **United** is the first airline to introduce a credit card (called "United Personal Travel Credit Card").

1973   **United** unveils AFIS (Air Freight Information System), the industry's most advanced system for tracing lost and mishandled bags.

1974   **United** introduces commercial aviation's first automated ticketing system, providing faster service for travel agencies and commercial accounts.

1981   **United** launches its Mileage Plus® frequent flyer program.

1994   **United** becomes the first airline to offer electronic tickets (E-Ticket℠).

1997   **United** partners with Air Canada, Lufthansa, SAS, and Thai International to create the Star Alliance.

1999   **United** Economy Plus℠ provides additional legroom for the airline's most frequent flyers in the economy section.

1999   **United** becomes the first U.S. airline to offer first-class customers a seat that converts into a bed.

2000   **United** equips its entire fleet with defibrillators to help passengers who suffer heart rhythm disturbances inflight.

2001   **United** Easy Check-in℠ kiosks are one part of the most comprehensive deployment ever of airport innovations designed to make travel faster and easier.

Margaret Hansen

Solomon Adio

Monika Miethke

Marilyn Thompson

Petra Janes

Dave Anderson

Bill Norwood

Luis Manon

Kristin Smith

Every so often I ask myself, 'What kind of a personality is United Air Lines?'
Then I remind myself that we are corporate citizens in more than 100 cities along our system.
We have the same civic obligations in each of them as do individual citizens.

–W. A. PATTERSON

ABOVE AND BEYOND | 217

UNITED AIRLINES IS A BUSINESS, TO BE SURE, BUT ITS DIVERSE AND TALENTED PEOPLE HAVE ALWAYS BEEN COMMITTED to more than a purely economic bottom line. In fact the company's commitment to corporate philanthropy and community sponsorships extends around the globe. Many of these activities take advantage of United's unique capabilities as a global airline and involve both employees and customers.

United rewards volunteerism among its more than 107,000 employees. The airline helps in many ways, including altering work schedules to make volunteerism easier. The United Airlines Foundation encourages individual efforts to improve and enrich the communities where employees live and work. Its philanthropic support flows through efforts that focus on arts and culture, corporate volunteerism, employee giving, humanitarian relief, and customer involvement programs such as the Mileage Plus Charity Miles and onboard coin collection programs. When the passion runs deep, United people often approach the company for help through a variety of employee-run programs. United's Civic Affairs group supports employee-driven efforts such as United We Care Employee Charitable Giving and employee volunteer programs, The United Airlines Employee Relief Fund, Take Your Community To Work Day, and Fantasy Flight, holiday parties held onboard for critically ill and disadvantaged children and their families.

As individuals, United employees are dedicated to the company, but also to people next door, in the next county, even a world away. Their charitable activities are most often private matters, marked by a quiet "thank you," a canceled check, or a prized snapshot. The following are just a few of the United people who are making a difference.

To encourage and reward employees who give of themselves, United's employee newsletter and inflight magazine have singled out those who embody the company's charitable spirit. Here are a few of their stories.

A Mother for the Girls / As a child, Margaret Hansen dreamed of a jet-setting life as an international flight attendant. Her 35-year career making customers comfortable on United flights has allowed her to live that dream. Of the places Hansen has called home, she always returns to Guatemala and the Para Las Niñas—For the Girls—orphanage where 27 orphan girls run to greet her at the door. For 11 years, Hansen has been the mother these little girls never had. She mastered Spanish to qualify for United's flight to Guatemala City. Even while based in London and Hong Kong, and later during months of chemotherapy following cancer surgery, she still made the long trips to Antigua and continues to do so. Some of the girls have families who visit once a month,

ORBIS

United's early support of the ORBIS flying eye hospital literally got the philanthropic enterprise off the ground. That visionary approach has helped ORBIS restore sight to thousands of people in developing countries around the world.

EYES IN THE SKIES / Some of United's good works are married to the business of flying. One such example is called ORBIS.

There are more than 40 million blind people in the world and 10 times that many suffer from disorders that may eventually cause them to lose sight permanently. In many cases there are procedures and tools available that could prevent blindness or restore sight, even to some who have never seen. The problem is that these medical miracles often do not find their way to the medical personnel who can put them to the best use—those in developing or impoverished parts of the world.

Since bringing medical people to the learning centers was a practical impossibility, a group formed in the United States to promote the idea of outfitting an airplane as an ophthalmologic teaching hospital and then flying it anywhere it was welcome. They called the effort Project ORBIS. While the concept was solid, the group had little money and, most notably, no airplane.

ORBIS leaders appealed to several airlines for help but came away empty-handed. Then they received an invitation to Chicago in 1978 to explain to United CEO Edward E. Carlson how a flying teaching hospital would work.

"I was pretty skeptical," Carlson said. "But the more I listened, the more impressed I became."

As the meeting went on, the UAL executive recalled a long-ago mentor, a father figure whose eyesight so deteriorated as he aged that he became nearly blind.

"I watched him age, and I watched him go through this and thought how unfortunate it was. He had a good life, but he could have had a better one if he had decent eye treatment."

Carlson said he would consider the request. Then he checked the fleet inventory. N8003U, a

DC-8 delivered in 1959, was sitting on a back ramp at Las Vegas International Airport gathering dust.

United agreed to donate the plane to the cause if the ORBIS team could come up with the money and equipment to turn it into a hospital. It was one of the oldest DC-8s, but to the ORBIS people it was a thing of beauty. The ORBIS team transformed the old jetliner. To accomplish its teaching mission, the aircraft also featured a classroom with video monitors linked to the operating room. United gave the volunteer ORBIS pilots several weeks of training in operating DC-8s. And once the jet was airworthy, United's maintenance base in San Francisco made it flight-ready.

In 1982, ORBIS, gleaming white with a stylized blue eye logo on its tail fin, departed for Panama, the first stop in what would become a decade of missions to some of the neediest places on earth. Everywhere the airplane went in Africa, Asia, and Central and South America, ORBIS was greeted with a kind of wonder. Time and again, patients would enter blind, and days later when the bandages came off, the world came into view. Local doctors and nurses got to "scrub in" and learn from some of the world's most accomplished surgeons, all ORBIS volunteers.

After 10 years of service to the world, ORBIS needed a larger aircraft. An intensive fundraising campaign purchased a used DC-10, and when the wide-bodied plane began its missions in 1994, the old DC-8 was finally retired. United continues to support ORBIS by donating services and travel for personnel, and United pilots are among today's ORBIS volunteers.

Whether United employees are supporting company-sponsored charitable efforts or pursuing projects that hold personal meaning, they truly demonstrate how the power of flight is changing the world. *///*

At right (clockwise from upper left) *the ORBIS flying eye hospital is christened in 1982; United's Jim Takeuchi* (L) *presents the DC-8 to Tony Zuma of ORBIS; the layout of the ORBIS interior; and the aircraft in flight.*

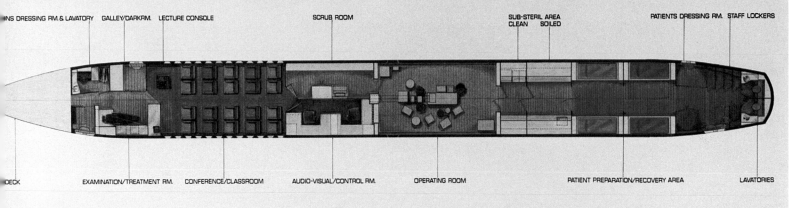

NS DRESSING RM. & LAVATORY   GALLEY/DARKRM.   LECTURE CONSOLE   SCRUB ROOM   SUB-STERIL AREA   PATIENTS DRESSING RM.   STAFF LOCKERS

CLEAN   SOILED

DECK   EXAMINATION/TREATMENT RM.   CONFERENCE/CLASSROOM   AUDIO-VISUAL/CONTROL RM.   OPERATING ROOM   PATIENT PREPARATION/RECOVERY AREA   LAVATORIES

United volunteers support an extraordinary array of organizations with their time and resources. And what happens when there isn't an organized group to support? Dozens of United employees have followed their hearts and founded their own.

and it's devastating for those who do not. Hansen is there to mend their broken hearts. "We do mother-and-daughter things," Hansen says, remembering the day she walked arm-in-arm with one girl at her secretarial school graduation. "They've all been abandoned, and I promised to stay in their lives," she says. "The most important thing I can do is keep coming back. My job at United lets me do that."

High Expectations / Nigerian immigrant Solomon Adio dreamed of flying as a boy. He grew up near an airport, and the lure of airplanes drew him to the United States and a career in aviation. Adio works as a United mechanic and helps keep United's aircraft flying safely. He also operates a flight school and trains pilots, many of whom become professionals. As a teacher, Adio realized he had something to share with the community. He developed a flight training program that helps at-risk youths in the San Francisco Bay–area find careers in aviation. "At $70 per flight hour, hands-on experience would otherwise be out of reach for these 14- to 18-year-old students," he says. "But it's the experience of flight that can motivate them to change their lives."

Powerful Medicine / Monika Miethke is a weightlifter, a United international flight attendant, and a breast cancer survivor. Miethke often talks publicly about her efforts to cope with the disease and life after cancer. Equally important is the inner strength she shares as the subject of the TV documentary *Breast Cancer and Recovery: A Personal Story.* Sharing her struggle—and her passion for exercise—was part of the healing process as well as preparation for a return to her job, a strenuous occupation that she does best when she's fit. The video, written and directed by a friend, was a labor of love to benefit The Breast Cancer Fund, a Bay-area nonprofit organization.

Redesigning Woman / Marilyn Thompson spends each day at United looking for new and more-effective ways to do business. As a project team leader she brings qualified people together to solve problems and find better ways to get jobs done. Although United's customers will likely never meet her, Thompson's work touches them each time they travel with United. Thompson uses the same skills to help Uptown Habitat for Humanity, a nonprofit builder of low-cost housing. As president of the board for the organization's Chicago affiliate, Thompson oversees construction projects that make the dream of home ownership a reality for low-income families. United added its support to a project that rebuilt several buildings on a block to help reinvent a neighborhood. "I don't change people," says Thompson. "At United, and at Habitat, we're just freeing people to come up with creative solutions to their own challenges."

Perfect Vision / Petra Janes eagerly embraces the challenges in her life. Nothing slows her down, least of all her blindness. With the aid of a Braille display, Janes assists customers with international travel plans as a United Airlines reservations representative. She's been a friendly, reassuring, and enthusiastic voice throughout her 18-year career. The feather in her cap was an appointment to Denver Mayor Wellington Webb's Commission for People with Disabilities. The group meets with individuals and agencies in the disabled community to help effect change on their behalf.

Ensuring the Eyes Have It / As a pilot for United Airlines, Dave Anderson understands the importance of clear vision. There's nothing quite like the view from the cockpit, and it's a view Anderson enjoys every day he goes to work as a Boeing 767 First

Officer. But sight is not a luxury he takes for granted. As the founder of Second Sight for Sore Eyes, an eyeglass donation project to benefit the people of Thailand, he also helps others see, many for the first time. Anderson and his wife, Siriwan, a native of Thailand, launched the program. The Andersons were vacationing in Thailand when they saw a newspaper article about a physician who matched up secondhand glasses with rural children who need them. "He was largely dependent on donated glasses," Anderson says. "I knew right then I wanted to help." He came home and started his program with glasses donated by United employees. Then civic organizations stepped up. Delivery was the biggest hurdle, but United flies to Bangkok. With help from employees on both sides of the Pacific and Star Alliance partner Thai International, the project has distributed thousands of serviceable eyeglasses free of charge. "For some of the school kids," says Anderson, "it makes the difference between learning to read and just waiting for the bell."

Man of Influence / Retired Captain Bill Norwood, a 26-year veteran with United Airlines, built a career around being first. He was United's first African-American captain and welcomes opportunities to share his story with children and to speak to them about the importance of education. Despite the demands of his career, Norwood worked to improve education and employment opportunities for minorities and students. He has served on Southern Illinois University's board of trustees and various boards designed to enhance educational opportunities for minorities.

Where Charity Begins / Luis Manon believes charity begins at home. While many United employees worked to provide relief to survivors of devastating Caribbean hurricanes in 1999, the efforts of Manon, a native of the hard-hit Dominican Republic, hit home with fellow employees. "Can you imagine waking up and not knowing where your child is, not having a roof over your head?" he asks. As a service director at one of the world's busier airports, Chicago O'Hare, Manon coordinates and supports United's front-line customer service employees. His attention to detail and customer focus helped him launch and then coordinate a relief effort for his homeland that became larger than he could have imagined. United donated a DC-10 freighter aircraft, and employees supported the airlift on their own time. "As an airline, we were in a unique position to help," he says.

Happy Camper / Everyone knows someone like Los Angeles–based flight attendant Kristin Smith—energetic, enthusiastic, and eternally optimistic. Smith's effusive personality is just what the doctor ordered for the children she works with at summer camps for kids with serious medical conditions ranging from congenital heart disease to severe burns and cancer. She got started through her mom's teaching physical education to mentally or physically challenged children. "I noticed that the kids she taught seemed different," she says. Her flexible schedule has permitted her to do many jobs, including serve as a camp director. Smith's camp experiences are at the same time heartening and heart-wrenching. Each season she looks forward to seeing familiar faces and meeting new youngsters—even though each camper represents a child afflicted with a serious medical condition. "These camps are vital to the kids' healing process because they give them a place where they can be treated like other kids," she says. When she started, a psychologist at a camp for severely burned children cautioned her about what she'd see. "But just like my mom said," she remembers, "I looked into their eyes and just saw that they were special."

Special—like thousands of United employees who do good works every day. _III_

UNITED ...ed to arrive at 2:26pm. This aircraft represents flig...

Houston

Scheduled departure **3:17**pm

On Time

Fli...

Air...

Du...

Mil...

Se...

Attention:

...customers with the following seat assignments ...hould remain in the gate area for a possible ...pgrade: 06F, 05F

Th...

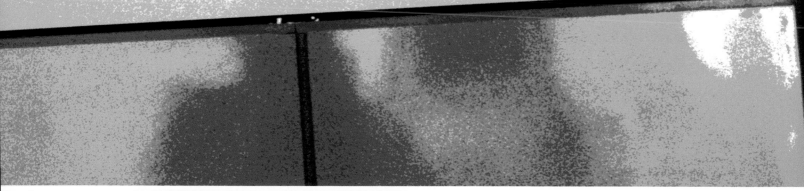

009 to Houston departing at 3:17pm. 2:11pm.

Flight 1009 / **SAS** 3939

Information

Airbus 319

of Flight: 2 hours, 44 minutes

Plus Miles: 925 miles

snack, audio

craft is configured for Economy Plus seating.

After working at United for more than 10 years, I'm surprised at how amazed I was while photographing a single plane over a 24-hour-period. It was a stunning reminder how much effort it takes to achieve what the public and even employees take for granted. It's a daily, ever-changing epic for each of the 600-plus planes we fly.

—MICHAEL P. MASUKA, UNITED PHOTOGRAPHER

5 a.m. Eastern Standard Time / IN THE DARKNESS OF THE EARLY MORNING, ORLANDO INTERNATIONAL AIRPORT IS deceptively quiet. Great airplanes sit on the tarmac as if posing for a still life. Inside the terminal, the ticket counters, waiting areas, and shops are deserted. In the luggage claim areas, carousels that will soon begin delivering thousands of bags are a frozen metal river. Occasionally a small truck speeds across the tarmac. But within hours, this airport will be an engine of activity.

Sitting silently on a corner of the tarmac is United's aircraft No. 4015, an Airbus 319, FAA registration number N815UA. It arrived in Orlando from Washington, DC, just after midnight. The lights in the plane are off, although the cockpit, officially known as the flight deck, is heated to keep the sophisticated instruments warm. This is one of 604 United aircraft that, within the next 24 hours, will make 2,329 scheduled flights flying 226,038 passengers to 130 destinations in 27 countries and two U.S. territories. It is one of United's 40 A319s. This particular aircraft was delivered on August 11, 1998, in Toulouse, France. Since that day it has completed 3,176 cycles—a takeoff and landing comprise a cycle—and spent 9,129 hours (more than a year) in the air.

Monday, January 22, 2001, is a typical day in the life of this airplane. It will spend slightly more time in the air than the nine hours daily that United's small airliners average. It begins the day designated United flight 1502, Orlando to Washington Dulles Airport, scheduled to depart at 7:15 a.m. By the time the sun rises on a clear morning, preparations are well under way.

6:05 a.m. / The catering truck delivers 86 breakfasts—eight first-class egg sandwiches, 77 croissants, and one special fruit plate.

6:10 a.m. / The plane is loaded with 16,000 pounds of aviation fuel for the 690-mile flight. The A319's three tanks each can hold as much as 14,000 pounds of fuel, which weighs about seven pounds per gallon. Aviation fuel is measured in pounds because all calculations necessary for a safe takeoff are determined by the weight of the aircraft. After checking the weather en route to DC and the scheduled passenger and freight loads—and knowing from experience that heavy air traffic in the DC area might cause some delays—the pilot, Captain Spike Hickman, decides to add another 1,000 pounds.

6:12 a.m. / Flight 1502 is coming alive. Two members of the ground crew begin loading the freight. Earlier that morning, mail going to DC had been picked up at the Orlando post office and will be delivered by United to a Washington, DC, post office.

6:15 a.m. / The crew arrives. First Officer Sara Fitch begins the outside walk-around, a visual examination of the plane that scrutinizes everything from the filaments in the headlights to the tires. Inside, the purser and two flight attendants complete the mandatory safety inspection and then begin preparations in the galley.

Keeping the Airbus safely in the air an average of nine hours a day requires the combined efforts of hundreds of people on the ground.

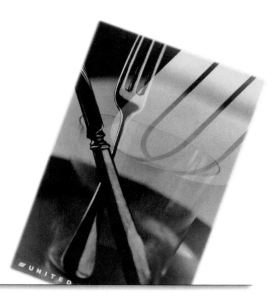

This "Airbus to Everywhere" gives new meaning to the blur of travel—6,432 miles, five cities, one of them twice, and 409 passengers in 24 hours. The result—the endlessly ongoing enterprise that is modern aviation.

6:50 a.m. / The first passengers come aboard. On the flight deck, Captain Hickman begins loading data into the computer. The A319 is among the most sophisticated airplanes in existence. The computerized autopilot, nicknamed "George," is not only capable of flying the plane, but can intercede if the pilot makes an error—for example, slows down to an unsafe speed.

7:15 a.m. / After passengers are seated, Purser Francis Bouffard welcomes them, making sure they are on the right flight and directing their attention to a preflight video on safety procedures. A tug pushes the aircraft away from the gate.

7:29 a.m. / The sun shines brightly as Captain Hickman taxis into takeoff position. One minute later, flight 1502—carrying 85 passengers, two pilots, and three flight attendants—rises from the ground into the morning sky, climbing to smooth air at 37,000 feet. Captain Hickman, who has been flying since 1963, was hired by United in 1991. First Officer Fitch, one of about 1,000 female pilots at the airline, learned to fly from her father, a Pan Am pilot, and soloed in a small plane before she drove a car.

Pilots and the flight crew bid for trips or are assigned to them based on seniority. Pilots' salaries vary based on seniority, the size and type of plane being flown, and which seat—captain, first officer, or engineer—they occupy. Crews often come together for a single flight and never work together again. Hickman and Fitch met at Newark Airport to begin their trip two days earlier and will stay together until returning to Newark Tuesday morning. On this cycle they will fly five airplanes to five cities.

8:50 a.m. / Hickman and Fitch go through the checklist to prepare for landing. The plane is flying IFR, instrument flight rules, which means that their movements are dictated by Air Traffic Controllers, "but in this case," Hickman explains, "it means 'I Follow Roads.' We're going to follow I-95 practically to the airport."

9:05 a.m. / Flight 1502 touches down at Dulles. Eight minutes later, the plane docks at the gate and passengers exit. The plane was marshaled in—guided into the gate—by Karl Franz, who directed Hickman by waving orange wands. Franz, a 16-year United veteran, is an aircraft mechanic. Franz chocks the wheels and conducts the arrival walk-around inspection, looking for any obvious damage, tire wear, hydraulic leaks, or jet fan blade damage. Almost immediately luggage and pressurized cargo holds are unloaded and the contents piled onto a three-car train of curtained carriers pulled by a tractor. Unlike a widebodied aircraft, where the cargo hold is big enough for cargo containers, the narrowbodied Airbus must be loaded and unloaded manually. Baggage handlers usually wear kneepads because they do not have room to stand up inside the hold.

9:16 a.m. / Hickman and Fitch leave the airplane, which is now United flight 1964, nonstop to Hartford, Connecticut's Bradley

Five separate teams flew the Airbus during this 24-hour period, from palm trees to snow, sunrise through sunset, across the United States.

Field, scheduled to depart at 11 a.m. After the last passengers exit, a four-person cleaning crew boards to clean the cabin. "People leave wallets all the time," says Candy Dayton, head of the crew. "We find glasses, cameras, credit cards, laptops, keys. One time somebody left an artificial leg." After a normal flight, the crew leaves the plane with four plastic bags of trash in tow.

10 a.m. / Flight Attendants Yvette Christiansen and Lyn Volz arrive and immediately begin preparations. They left Chicago at 6 this morning. Christiansen flies this Chicago-Washington, DC-Hartford-Chicago route three times a week, which allows her to be home by 2:30 p.m. Her 22-year-old daughter, Carla, is also a United flight attendant. "I pinned on her wings," Yvette says proudly, "and I was crying. We've only flown together once." Volz has been flying for four years and lacks the seniority to "hold" the trips of her choice, so most often she flies "reserve," meaning the scheduling department simply assigns her to flights.

10:05 a.m. / The Dobbs catering truck trailer is hydraulically lifted to the service door. Normally the staff removes the empty service carts and replenishes them with the precise number of meals ordered for the next flight, but this 49-minute hop to Hartford will serve only beverages.

10:15 a.m. / First Officer Tony Stella conducts the preflight walk-around, again checking for external damage or wear. The walk-around is always conducted the same way, circling the entire aircraft from the left front around the nose, then to the rear and around the tail. Stella checks pressure indicators on the tires and inspects the brakes for evidence of rust. He also checks the blade tips and the soft rubber spinner (the cone at the center of the fan blades) for damage, and he checks the hollow tubes that measure air speed. Ten minutes later, Stella completes the check, satisfied that the plane is in good flying condition.

10:20 a.m. / Pilot Gary Zientara boards the plane. "I grew up near an airport and a train switching station," he says, "so I wanted to be either an astronaut or a train engineer. I became a pilot—it was halfway between the two."

10:30 a.m. / The lavatory service truck arrives and empties the lavatory tanks.

11:08 a.m. / Flight 1964 takes off and rapidly climbs 29,000 feet into the clear blue Washington, DC, sky. The light load of 17 passengers is spread sparsely throughout the cabin. On the flight deck Zientara is sitting in the captain's seat and Stella is on his right. Between them, on the control panel and above, an array of dials and computer readouts report the progress of the plane. The flight controls are duplicated for the captain and first officer and will work independently or together. The captain flies the plane with a "stick" held in his left hand; the first officer flies with his right hand. George, the autopilot (legend has it that the name comes from the expression "Let George do it") is actually flying the aircraft, and when Air Traffic Control directs them to change altitude, Zientara adjusts a dial and George smoothly makes the adjustment.

The people change but the routine doesn't. Pilots and first officers use the same words to communicate with Air Traffic Control. When one of them informs ATC, "The field is in sight" (meaning that he sees the airport), the other responds affirmatively, "I have it." Back in the cabin, equipment is stowed in exactly the same place in every A319.

Many employees remain loyal to Boeing, who supplied United with its planes for decades—including its earliest mail and passenger planes in the 1920s and '30s. "If it ain't Boeing, I ain't going," they laughingly singsong, but the A319 has quickly established a reputation as an extraordinary aircraft. Zientara has the seniority to fly the much bigger 747-400, "but I like this airplane too much."

11:35 a.m. / As the plane begins descending into Hartford's Windsor-Locks, Bradley International Airport, Stella blocks the blinding rays of the morning sun with a transparent yellow shade. Stella's uncle flew for USAir, which is where Stella caught his

passion for flight. The first time his 3-year-old son flew, he looked around the cockpit and said to his father, "So this is your office."

As the plane drops below 10,000 feet, all conversation in the cockpit not specifically related to the safety of the aircraft ceases, as mandated by FAA regulations. Regularly, a mechanical voice announces the number of feet above the ground in deep elongated tones, like a tape recorder running just a bit too slowly, "Twenty-five hundred," and below until the plane touches down at 12:04 p.m. When it reaches the gate, the pilots quickly run through another checklist, then shut down its two engines.

Seconds after the jets whine to a stop, the ground crew goes to work. The ideal time to turn around a narrowbody aircraft is 40 minutes, 50 minutes for a widebody, but events often make that impossible. This will be a brief stop, so the plane is cleaned quickly by two customer service agents rather than a cleanup crew. On the tarmac, in the crisp 27-degree temperature of snowy Hartford, a ramp service employee does a walk-around inspection. Within minutes the luggage and cargo from Dulles are unloaded, bags and shipments bound for Chicago and Houston are loaded. Members of the ground crew normally work between four and 10 flights during their eight-hour shift. Food handlers have stored the 120 meals, and the fueler has added the 9,800 pounds of fuel requested by Zientara.

Once the passengers have deplaned, an aircraft maintenance technician comes aboard, as he does after each landing, to check the plane's logbook. Flight 1964 has been perfect, so Captain Zientara has made no comments. If the pilot had described any problems, the mechanic would be responsible for resolving them as rapidly as possible. If there is a potential safety problem, he can elect to keep the plane grounded until it is repaired. An inspection of the logbook reveals that N815UA's problems have all been minor: "Seat 2B, C Pax control unit will not change channels." "Seat 1B will not stay upright." "Capt earpiece attachment fitting missing." The plane keeps flying, nine hours a day, every day, an endlessly repeated cycle of takeoffs and landings, but there is never a moment when it is not being carefully maintained. In addition to the normal checks done following each landing, more-extensive maintenance is scheduled monthly and annually, leading up to a complete overhaul—a D-check—that takes place after 2,918 days in operation.

The Airbus A319 ages slowly. Pilots report that the planes are usually in continuous operation for several years before they begin to notice nicks, dings, and scratches, most of which are easily repaired, and it will take as long as 15 years before they expect to see "slop," a looseness in the controls. That's years away for what's now become United flight 1009, from Hartford to Houston, with a stopover in Chicago. It will be a full flight; all eight first-class and 112 seats of Economy Plus and coach will be filled.

12:35 p.m. / As the passengers begin boarding, Flight Attendant Ellen Grant prepares the food service. First-class passengers will choose between filet mignon or pasta primavera, and the other passengers will receive a snack box containing a roast beef sandwich, potato or macaroni salad, and a raspberry cheesecake bar.

1:05 p.m. / The Airbus is pushed away from the gate by a tug, taking off for Chicago's O'Hare at 1:25 p.m. As far as the passengers are concerned, this plane's day has just begun and it will end when it lands in Chicago. They don't know that it has already completed two flights. N815UA is plowing through another day, fed by a continuous flow of pilots, flight attendants, and passengers.

Passengers can use free headsets to listen to 10 channels of audio programming, including channel 9—Air Traffic Control. United is the only U.S. airline to let customers listen in on communications between the control tower and airplanes, where they can hear the tower order, "Cleared for takeoff, runway 32 left," and can even hear about the occasional weather delay before the announcement is made by the pilot.

The Airbus speeds through the sky at Mach .81, 440 knots, which is about 480 miles per hour. The 120 passengers bound for Chicago aboard flight 1009 are a typical cross-section of the flying public. Milvia DiBrino of Waterbury, Connecticut, smiles brightly as she explains that her daughter, "the doctor," will meet her at O'Hare and together they will fly to Las Vegas, "where I intend to win!" Sitting in the rear of the Airbus are Liz Beinhauer, her 2-year-old son, Ethan, and her mother, Mary Peterson, who have been visiting Hartford to celebrate the 86th birthday of Ethan's great-grandmother. Three seats forward is Beverly Griffith, on her way home to Denver following the funeral of her father. Sister Mary of the Immaculate Conception, wearing her white nun's habit, explains that she is en route to a meeting of the planning committee for the 16 Dominican monasteries in the United States.

2:13 p.m. Central Standard Time / Flight 1009 lands in Chicago. The temperature at O'Hare is a cool 30 degrees. Seconds after the passenger loading bridge is locked in place against the door, several knocks are heard. Until recently, flight attendants responded with a "thumbs up" signal through the small window, but that was changed to a return knock when it was discovered that in certain cultures the thumbs-up gesture is offensive. As the door opens, a customer service representative enters.

"Specials?" he asks, meaning are there any passengers aboard requiring special treatment—unaccompanied minors, people needing assistance, or passengers who do not speak English.

"None," is the answer. The passengers begin leaving the airplane. Shortly thereafter, mechanic Charles DiTomassi, a 13-year United veteran, boards and checks the log. While he is in the cockpit, the caterers arrive to cart away empty trays and stock the plane. Because 1009 is a through-flight, meaning it stops in Chicago rather than ends there, the cleaning staff is responsible for the lavatories but the flight attendants clean the cabin. This is the end of the trip for the Chicago-based crew.

2:40 p.m. / Captain G. Kirk Hansen slides into the left-hand seat occupied less than an hour ago by a pilot whose name he's never even heard. First Officer Dave Pletcher, who met Hansen for the first time the day before when they started their trip in a snowstorm, concludes his walk-around and arrives minutes later. Coincidentally, Hansen and Pletcher flew this same aircraft yesterday, although they might never fly it again. While Pletcher begins his preflight check, Hansen confers with Flight Attendant Don Kolcheff, going over the weather reports, and the number of knocks that will tell him when a crew member needs access to the flight deck. "One of the most important things," Kolcheff explains with a laugh, "is when the pilots want to eat."

2:55 p.m. / Passengers bound for Houston begin boarding. It's a scene repeated thousands of times every day on United—passengers searching for their seats, lifting baggage into the overhead compartments, making last-minute calls on their mobile phones. After checking the weather en route to Houston, the passenger load, and the fact that the plane will be carrying 2,800 pounds of baggage, mail, and freight—bringing the total weight of the plane at takeoff to 134,000 pounds—Hansen adds 12,000 pounds of fuel.

3:20 p.m. / Flight 1009 is pushed back from the gate to join the line of aircraft waiting to take off. "It's a beautiful day to fly," Hansen says softly. He's been flying for 37 years, including a stint flying army helicopters in Vietnam. "There have been so many days and nights I'll never forget," he says, his eyes gleaming with memories. "One night about four years ago, it was midnight and we were halfway across the Atlantic. Out of the right side of the aircraft I could see a full lunar eclipse, directly in front of me was the Hale-Bopp comet moving across the sky, and on my left I could see the aurora borealis. It was extraordinary—like I was sitting in the largest planetarium in the universe."

Over the intercom, the tower reminds the pilots, "Keep the line tight, please. Move on up." Ten minutes later the controller says, "Cleared for takeoff. Runway two-one north. Turn left two-seven-zero," meaning that the plane is to make a left turn when airborne. Minutes later flight 1009 is back in the air, climbing to 35,000 feet, and heading for Houston.

Although 34-year-old First Officer Dave Pletcher is 24 years younger than Hansen, he actually has more experience flying A319s. But airlines honor seniority, and that means Captain Hansen has full responsibility for this aircraft, although he will happily depend on Pletcher for advice. Before setting foot on the flight deck of an Airbus, both men had five weeks of intensive training—the longest training period of all United's schools—in Airbus simulators. "The full-motion simulators are incredibly realistic," Pletcher says. Once a year pilots return to the training center for a complete review and are subjected to an extraordinary variety of emergencies in the simulator. "Just about all the problems we could possibly encounter up here we've already dealt with in the simulator," says Pletcher.

4 p.m. / Flight Attendant Charlotte Graham begins preparing the food service. Graham has been flying 11 years for United. "Three years ago I was on a six-person DC-10 crew to Europe that represented an incredible range of nationalities. I'm African-American, and we had a Pakistani, a Puerto Rican, an Asian, and a Serb, so we decided to have a potluck dinner. We each brought a representative dish to eat."

A strong tailwind pushes the Airbus all the way to Houston. After months of rough weather, four high-pressure areas have created blue skies from coast to coast, border to border. "You don't get many like this," Hansen says appreciatively.

5:37 p.m. / Flight 1009 completes its journey to Houston, Texas. The sun is just beginning to set on the day. At gate A-10 inside the airport, a customer service representative announces to passengers waiting to board flight 377 to Los Angeles that the plane is now on the ground. Within the allotted 40 minutes, all remnants of flight 1009 have disappeared, its existence reduced to a pile of reports: how many people, how many bags, how much freight, and, as always throughout the long history of United, how many pounds of mail were delivered.

In many ways, N815UA is simply a highly sophisticated, multimillion dollar carrying case. It's a machine that just keeps moving to no permanent destination. It has no home base; it flies toward no end point. Its parts will be replaced before they are worn or when they are damaged. At intervals, it will be torn apart and put back together. It will be flown until it is no longer economically feasible, and when it is discarded no person will mourn its passing. It will carry tens of thousands of passengers millions of miles, and it will be flown by countless pilots who will not know from where it came or where it is going next. Thousands of flight attendants will serve tens of thousands of meals, and it will be cleaned and refueled four, five, six times a day, every day. It's a workhorse. A magnificent, reasonably comfortable, efficient workhorse.

In Houston, flight 377 is born. For months, while people made reservations to fly to Los Angeles on this day at this time, it has existed only as a number on paper. The plane was assigned to the flight number only weeks earlier. And within hours of landing in Los Angeles, the flight will again exist only on paper.

6:30 p.m. / The passengers begin boarding as another cycle starts. Normally this flight is at least three-quarters full, and often it carries a full load, but for some reason tonight only 22 passengers are aboard. Noting this light load, Captain Ken Carlson adds only 2,000 pounds of fuel. Twenty-two meals are loaded, among them five special orders: two Muslim meals, two vegetarian, and one Hindu. Carlson joined United 11 years ago after 20 years in the Air Force, ending his military career as a major. "This is my

237

Flight Attendant Khoi Evans starts off the early Orlando-Washington, DC, flight with beverage service—hot coffee mostly.

In 24 hours, the Airbus has flown a web of routes. "Until that trip," says United's Mick Masuka, "I never grasped the countless lives United touches in 640 such marathons a day. Amazing."

retirement job," he says. Both Carlson and First Officer Chris Strand are based in Los Angeles and will be going home after a four-day trip that took them from Los Angeles to Philadelphia, Chicago, Vancouver, Denver, Houston, and back to LAX.

Night falls while the plane is on the ground in Houston. Lights are now burning brightly all around the airport.

6:55 p.m. / Flight 377 rises into the night. The three flight attendants agree that they prefer working a more crowded plane; it makes the flight seem quicker. Among the three of them, they have 37 years of experience. With awe they note that the record-holder is Los Angeles–based Flight Attendant Ron Akana—one of the "Original Eight" stewards hired by United when the airline began flying to Hawai'i—who has 52 years of seniority.

Almost a third of United's 25,000 flight attendants are men. Two of flight 377's flight attendants, Phillip Brown and Benjamin Akin, have been "buddy bidding" (flying together) since meeting at United's training center 10 years earlier. "We bid lines to fly together," Brown explains. They like this particular trip—LA-Chicago-Houston-LA—because it accounts for 11 hours of flight time. Flight attendants must fly a minimum of 65 hours a month, although they are restricted by the FAA to a maximum of 265 flying hours quarterly. Like pilots, they bid for trips that fit their personal needs, but their ability to "hold" the trip they bid is based completely on seniority. None of the flight attendants knows if they have ever worked on this airplane before. The flight attendants begin beverage service as soon as the plane reaches its assigned altitude of 31,000 feet. The estimated flying time is three hours and nine minutes, just enough to serve a meal and show the inflight movie.

On the flight deck, George is in control, but Carlson and Strand both continuously scan the night in front of them. The visibility is almost 80 miles, and far ahead the blinking lights of two airplanes can be seen. When Strand leaves the cockpit for a moment, Carlson immediately puts on his oxygen mask as mandated by FAA regulations. Carlson much prefers flying in the daytime, when he can point out sights of interest to his passengers. He carries a large map of the United States with him that lists interesting sights and historic facts state-by-state. But, he explains, "On the Airbus the movie doesn't pause when I make an announcement like it does on some of the bigger aircraft, so I try not to bother them while they're watching the film."

8:18 p.m. Pacific Standard Time / It's 55 degrees in Los Angeles when the Airbus lands and glides into gate 71. Like actors in a long-running play, the ground crew goes to work. The customer service reps, mechanic, baggage handlers, caterers, and cleaners sweep through the plane like a passing storm. When a new crew is in place, N815UA has become flight 202, nonstop from Los

In the middle of a Washington, DC, night, the plane is bathed in deicing fluid. The frost vanishes, and soon the plane will be gone, too.

The workhorse Airbus is one of the modern miracles that has turned the achievement of commercial air travel into a mundane convenience. Though often taken for granted, it is nevertheless no small feat. Just another day leaping across a continent.

Angeles International Airport to Washington Dulles.

9:25 p.m. / Flight Attendant Gavin Sutphin, who has been flying for United for 35 years, begins the same safety check she has conducted countless times on countless aircraft. She makes sure all switches and controls are in the proper position, that the evacuation equipment is properly stowed, and the safety equipment is in the proper place. Then she checks two door gauges to verify the pressure levels of pressurized air canisters that will help open the door and inflate the emergency slide in an emergency. Gavin notes that the job has changed completely in her 35 years. "When I started we were gracious servers of food and beverages. Now we have to know how to deal with hijackers, give first aid, and recognize the components of a bomb."

In the cabin, Amy Disbarte and Jaime P. Chilson are helping passengers find their seats and stow their bags. The redeye, the overnight flight to DC, is considered an easy flight to work. Most of the 67 passengers will sleep through the night flight. Flight 202 connects with a Paris-bound flight, so after welcoming passengers in English, Sutphin repeats the greeting in French.

10:12 p.m. / Flight 202 takes off. Both Pilot Brad Smith and First Officer Jack Miller are on reserve for the month of January, meaning for 18 days during the month they can be assigned to any flight. The remaining days they are off. Scheduling called them at home yesterday afternoon to assign them to this flight. The men had never met before, but, Smith points out, "it wouldn't be any different if we'd worked together for years."

Also on the flight deck is Mike Bigelow, a United Express pilot hitching a ride back to his base in DC. Neither the pilots nor the flight attendants have to live in the city where they are based as long as they can get there in time to go to work. Many crew members commute to work via plane. Others drive. One United pilot commuted to his New York City base from his home in Sydney, Australia. The general rule is that there have to be at least two flights that will get you to your assignment in case the first is delayed or canceled.

The cabin is dark as the Airbus flies east into the morning at 37,000 feet. On the flight deck the first officer communicates with Air Traffic Control stations across the country. George is at work—blissfully unaware that one day is becoming another.

5:20 a.m. / Flight 202 lands at Dulles. It is 14 degrees, and the wind-chill factor is close to 0 degrees. The airport is as quiet as the flight has been. As the Airbus taxis to the gate, it passes silent United aircraft of all sizes ready for the day to begin.

5:30 a.m. / The bells inside the cabin chime and people stand up and stretch, collect their carryon luggage, and patiently leave the plane. No one says a word; it's too early in the morning for conversation.

But for this A319 the time of day is irrelevant. Since departing Orlando early yesterday morning, it has safely carried 409 passengers a total of 6,432 miles east, west, north, and south to five cities, twice to Washington, DC. As the Airbus sits on the tarmac before its next flight, frost collects on its wings and fuselage. Before passengers are permitted to board, deicing crews standing on cherry pickers spray the plane with bluish-green deicing fluid. The frost disappears. The plane is again as clean as it was when it left Orlando. The day is done, but the cycle continues.

6:36 a.m. / Airbus N815UA, now flight 399, departs for Denver, chased toward the Rockies by the dawn of a new day. *///*

WINGS OF TOMORROW

I confess that in 1901, I said to my brother Orville that man would not fly for fifty years. Ever since, I have distrusted myself and avoided predictions. —WILBUR WRIGHT

THE FUTURE OF FLIGHT

THROUGHOUT UNITED'S 75 YEARS, VISIONARIES HAVE LOOKED TO THE FUTURE. IN THE MIDST OF WORLD WAR II, United's advertising heralded the Age of Flight and predicted, "Tomorrow's planes will carry 10 times the freight, many times the passengers, and they will go to parts of the earth hidden from highways, ships, and railways."

By the end of the war, corporate executives were hedging just a bit. "Stories are told of 16-engined transports," read a press release, "that carry hundreds of persons and unnumbered tons of cargo across vast distances at speeds ranging from 500 to 1,000 miles per hour. United officials do not discount such prophecies for the distant future, but they paint no such colorful vision for the five years immediately following the war."

In 1961, United offered employees a $25 bond for predicting what air travel might be like 35 years in the future—in 1996. The winner was R.J. O'Leary of the San Francisco ticket office who predicted, "With Tokyo or Paris only 1–2 hours from the U.S., it has become operationally and economically necessary to effect a merger with a major intercontinental carrier. Now our Tokyo-New York passengers dispense with the annoying change of planes in San Francisco.

"The normal flight altitude of the DC-32 is 150,000 feet with a true airspeed of Mach 4.... With the high speed of the DC-32 there's no time for meal service as known in 1961. But Passenger Service reports enthusiastic reception of the new built-in seat-back 'snack bar,' an encapsulated snack tray preloaded by Dining Service.... United now operates its own STOL [short take-off & landing] feeder aircraft. Embodying the best features of the helicopter and the limousine they conveniently transfer passengers from suburban areas to the airport.

The future may see aircraft like the Boeing Sonic Cruiser (left) or double-decker planes like those in United's 1943 ad series "The Age of Flight" (page 251). A Boeing 80A circa 1930 over Chicago (preceding pages).

"Everyone is familiar with United's 'Car-Go' Liners, which are especially popular with campers. Passengers merely load up the station wagon and drive to the airport where a skilled UAL agent drives their car into the cargo compartment and they go aboard the passenger section."

Third-place winner C.C. Janse-Kok, a Denver ticket sales agent, also looked into a crystal ball. "Behold the standard efficiency airport now in use in every major city in the United States. The only aboveground structure is the control tower. A traveler enters the subterranean terminal by escalator, elevator, declining walkway, or steps.

"Supersonic jetliners cross the continent in about an hour and are used only for trans- or intercontinental travel. Boeing and Douglas merged in 1971 to manufacture the first of the costly supersonic jetliners. We have all gotten used to the bat wing–like Rotavion jetliner, taking off vertically and cruising at 400 miles per hour."

In 1968, Harlan Gurney, who had flown the airmail routes and been an original United pilot, told an interviewer, "The supersonic is marvelous; it's going to come. But it's not going to hold a candle to subsonic transportation. That's where we should be giving most of our attention. The supersonic is sort of like whipped cream on a strawberry tart. Nice, but not essential."

In 1970, George Stuart, manager of system freight sales, predicted that delivery of air freight to outlying locations would be accomplished by some form of helicopter-freighter or "heli-freighter," which would air shuttle the containers directly to distribution centers in nearby cities. "Trucks will continue to service areas within a 100-mile radius."

And in 1966, Pat Patterson took a look into the future. Among the things he saw was a dubious future for a supersonic passenger plane. "Our government has to develop that plane to maintain this country's prestige in the field of air transportation ... but it's going to be a difficult plane to produce and operate.... We will have to charge a premium of at least 30 percent to fly on an SST [supersonic transport] and I doubt very much that people will pay for that. From what I can see most people want to fly at the lowest possible cost, even when it means accepting a lower class of service."

Patterson also predicted that a major problem facing the aviation industry would be congestion at airports. "The solution is more runways and widespread use of the new Instrument Landing System to bring planes in faster.... At Chicago we have a wonderful airport—O'Hare—but in a snowstorm we can only use one runway. If we had five parallel runways, properly separated, together with ILS, we could get planes in there even in the worst weather. And New York must have another airport somewhere. Los Angeles will need another one, too."

He saw developments on the horizon to make flying safer. "Someday we'll have a traffic control system with computers that will take charge when a plane is in danger of collision and make the necessary corrections automatically. That sounds pretty far-fetched, but it's coming."

And finally, when asked if rockets would ever be used to shoot people from place to place across the earth, he was reflective. "At my age [67] I won't say anything can't happen. When I consider the men that are whirling around the earth in spaceships and compare that with the flight Lindbergh made only 39 years ago, certainly the airlines will be using rockets someday."

Rockets may be the distant future, but the near future holds some pretty amazing planes. Both Boeing and its European rival, Airbus, are building super-long range jetliners capable of flying 17, 18, 19 hours and more. A 777 with a 22-hour endurance is in the works. That means airplanes will soon be able to fly nonstop almost halfway around the globe, the longest distance between any two points on earth.

Big things are on the horizon. Boeing is planning the Sonic Cruiser, a radical new high-speed jetliner able to cruise at nearly the speed of sound. That decision follows close on the heels of Airbus' unveiling the A380, a three-deck goliath with a takeoff weight exceeding 1 million pounds. Initially the aircraft will carry 555 passengers in three classes with enough room aboard for shops, restaurants, exercise and meeting rooms, and even separate sleeping quarters. Later versions are planned that can seat up to 800 people. Delivery date of the first version is 2006.

Whether or not such amenities find commercial application, passengers can expect future aircraft to provide extensive digital

New Horizons in the *Age of Flight*

THINK how far you might have traveled in the past . . . the places you might have visited . . . the people you might have met — *if only you could have spared the time.* Your viewpoint of the world you live in would have been broadened immeasurably.

Before air transport was developed, crossing the country took four or five days each way. Going to Europe meant nearly a week at sea, South America three weeks, the Orient a month.

The Age of Flight will demonstrate to everyone everywhere that time is no longer a major obstacle to travel. For each hour will carry you more miles than ever before.

No two cities anywhere in the United States will be more than a few hours apart. Frequent, regular airline service will take you to South America in a day, or across the Atlantic overnight.

Along with this greatly expanded air travel, *all* forms of transportation will have bigger responsibilities . . . new cargoes to carry . . . more people to serve.

And you will train your sights on a new world. All of its marvels will be brought within your reach. You will have new markets to sell . . . new goods to buy. You will see new horizons in the Age of Flight.

TIME-TABLE FOR THE AGE OF FLIGHT			
From	To	Air Miles	Today (or Tomorrow)
New York	San Francisco	2678	19¼ hrs. — 10 hrs.
Chicago	Singapore	9365	6½ days — 48 hrs.
Washington	Moscow	4883	51 hrs. — 21 hrs.
New York	London	3460	20 hrs. — 14 hrs.
Chicago	New York	747	4½ hrs. — 3 hrs.
Los Angeles	Seattle	1019	7½ hrs. — 4 hrs.
Portland	Philadelphia	2608	18¼ hrs. — 10 hrs.

★ *Buy War Bonds and Stamps for Victory* ★

UNITED
AIR LINES
THE MAIN LINE AIRWAY

services, including direct access to their office intranets. Time in the air may no longer mean time away from work.

Aircraft of the more distant future may look quite different from the ones we use today. In the late 1990s McDonnell Douglas was pursuing a new concept called the blended-wing body, in which the forward body blends into the wing in a single structure. The concept allows a significant reduction in power-robbing drag, lowers the weight, and enhances lift, making the aircraft far more efficient. This airliner's cabin would be wide enough to be divided into separate, side-by-side rooms. Boeing purchased McDonnell Douglas in 1997 and is still evaluating the concept.

And although the Concorde failed to achieve commercial success, it has demonstrated the desirability of supersonic travel. New technologies will surely solve the SST's vexing environmental problems, including sonic booms, approach noise, and unacceptable emissions. When that occurs, a new, larger SST is likely to emerge.

One way to solve nagging atmospheric challenges is to escape the atmosphere altogether. It is not inconceivable that future transports, possibly fueled by hydrogen, will launch from airports, zoom into low orbit, and transit the oceans at speeds of Mach 10. The distance between continents will be measured in minutes, not hours.

While such spaceplanes are a long way off, space itself is not. Efforts are under way to develop vehicles that can safely and profitably take paying passengers aloft for a brief visit into outer space. Such flights are technically achievable—and some say likely—in the first decades of the 2000s. And longer visits to space, once the stuff of science fiction, will surely happen, too. The International Space Station is making those dreams an everyday reality. Indeed, a Russian spacecraft took the first tourist into space in 2001.

It was not so long ago that the principal transcontinental conveyance was a Pullman car swaying behind a smoky steam locomotive and the only way to Hawai'i was by boat. United helped change those realities over just a few decades.

It's too soon to ask when you might catch a United flight to the moon for a vacation at the Sea of Tranquility. But people may indeed pose that question in a not-too-distant future. Going farther, faster, and in comfort is a tradition at United, and that's not likely to change in the years to come, whatever the destination.

If the past is a guide, the future is surely closer than we think. *///*

251

CREDITS

All photography and memorabilia in *The Age of Flight* courtesy of and © UA Archives, unless noted below.

Front of Book

pages 14-15 / UNITED (CREATIVE SERVICES) / photography

Early Years

page 18 . . . UA ARCHIVES, Gift of L.F. BISHOP / historical photography

page 19 . . . UA ARCHIVES, Gift of L.F. BISHOP / memorabilia

page 22 . . . UA ARCHIVES, Gift of JACK KNIGHT / memorabilia

page 25 . . . UA ARCHIVES, Gift of E. HAMILTON LEE / memorabilia

page 26 . . . UA ARCHIVES, Gift of C.T. WRIGHTSON / memorabilia

page 27 . . . UA ARCHIVES, Gift of C.T. WRIGHTSON / memorabilia

page 33 . . . UA ARCHIVES, Gift of L.D. CUDDEBACK / memorabilia

page 39 . . . UA ARCHIVES, Gift of L.F. BISHOP / memorabilia

page 42 . . . CORBIS / lower left, historical photography

page 49 . . . UA ARCHIVES, Gift of BERNICE JOHNSON / memorabilia

pages 52-53 . . . Gift of S.A. STIMPSON / memorabilia

page 55 . . . UA ARCHIVES, Gift of J.D. HUTCHINSON / memorabilia

page 61 . . . UA ARCHIVES, Gift of BETTY ROSE MIER CALLAHAN / memorabilia

page 64 . . . Courtesy VICY MORRIS YOUNG / memorabilia

page 73 . . . Courtesy DR. CHARLES C. QUARLES / memorabilia

page 80 . . . UA ARCHIVES, Gift of J.D. HUTCHINSON / memorabilia

Technological Achievements

page 85 . . . UA ARCHIVES, Gift of L.F. BISHOP / memorabilia

page 88 . . . UA ARCHIVES, Gift of UNITED AIRLINES HISTORICAL FOUNDATION / memorabilia

page 89 . . . UA ARCHIVES, Gift of WILLIAM DEPPNER & E.E. "BUCK" HILBERT / memorabilia

page 93 . . . JEPPESEN SANDERSON / historical photography

page 99 . . . UA ARCHIVES, Gift of S.A. STIMPSON / memorabilia

pages 106-107 . . . SMITHSONIAN INSTITUTION / historical photography

page 113 . . . CHRIS SORENSEN / photography

page 120 . . . UNITED (CREATIVE SERVICES) / photography

pages 122-123 . . . UNITED (CREATIVE SERVICES) / photography

pages 124-127 . . . ILLUSTRATION © RAYMOND E. SMITH

In the preparation of Raymond Smith's aircraft illustrations, we would like to thank CASEY SMITH (San Diego Aerospace Museum), MIKE LOMBARDY (Boeing Archives), PAT MCGINNIS (Douglas Archives), DENNIS PARKS (Seattle Museum of Flight), and BRIAN NICKLAS (Smithsonian's National Air & Space Museum), for their genuine interest in the history of aviation and the extra effort each contributed to share that passion with readers of this book.

pages 128-129 . . . UNITED (CREATIVE SERVICES) / photography

Selling the Sky

page 136 . . . UA ARCHIVES, Gift of HAROLD OGLE / memorabilia

page 139 . . . Courtesy MORGAN CARVER / HEMISPHERES cover "COUNTDOWN"

page 157 . . . POSTER BY JOSEPH FEHER / Gift of Pace Communications

pages 158-159 . . . UA ARCHIVES, Gift of G.C. GIMPLE / memorabilia

page 166 . . . (photography clockwise from top left) REAGAN LIBRARY; ELIZABETH MCCALL; JANICE HAMBLET; JANICE HAMBLET

pages 178-179 . . . Courtesy FALLON MCELLIGOTT

Going Global

pages 186-187, 189 . . . OXFORD CARTOGRAPHERS / maps

page 189 . . . (photography clockwise from top left) JAMES WHITLOW DELANO; PETRINA TINSLAY; JOSHUA PAUL; JAMES WHITLOW DELANO; BAA PICTURE LIBRARY

pages 190-191 . . . MIKE DUBOSE, The Tennessean / photography

page 193 . . . UA ARCHIVES, Gift of J.D. HUTCHINSON / memorabilia

page 195 . . . LILLIAN KEIL / photography

page 199 . . . COURTESY OF SOFIA PROJECT / illustration

pages 206-207.. . UNITED AIRLINES GENEALOGY / Corporate and Legal History of United Air Lines and Its Predecessors and Subsidiaries, Vols. 1 & 2, 1925-1955, 20th Century Press, Chicago, 1953; Minute books of the boards of directors of Varney, PAT, BAT, NAT, United Air Lines, Inc.; Moody's Manual of Investments, 1925-1934; Data supplied by the Office of the General Counsel, United Airlines / Copyright 1997 / Revised 4-20-01

pages 210-211 . . . CRAIG CAMPBELL & ASSOCIATES / United Services advertisement

page 213 . . . MICHAEL P. MASUKA / photography

page 215 . . . UNITED (CREATIVE SERVICES) / photography

page 216 . . . (photography clockwise from top left) SUSAN KASLAW-NELSON; JEROME MERIWEATHER; JEROME MERIWEATHER; JEROME MERIWEATHER; MICHAEL P. MASUKA; MICHAEL P. MASUKA; DON JISKRA, SUSAN KASLAW-NELSON; JEROME MERIWEATHER

page 219 . . . ORBIS / photography

A Day in the Life

pages 222-223 . . . MICHAEL P. MASUKA / photography

page 224 . . . CHRIS SORENSEN / photography

pages 226-227, 229 . . . MICHAEL P. MASUKA / photography

pages 230-231, 233, 236 . . . CHRIS SORENSEN / photography

pages 238-239 . . . MICHAEL P. MASUKA / photography

page 241 . . . CHRIS SORENSEN / photography

pages 242-243, 245 . . . MICHAEL P. MASUKA / photography

Wings of Tomorrow

page 248 . . . BOEING / photo-illustration

pages 249 . . . SMITHSONIAN INSTITUTION / historical photography

UNITED AIR LINES

Mr._____

Cab Leaves _____

Plane Leaves_____

Connecting ⟦**Plane**⟧ Lea
Return ⟦**Train**⟧

UNITE